PILLARS OF FIRE
IN MY SOUL

Pillars of Fire
in My Soul

Robert Stackpole, S.T.D., Editor

John Paul II Institute of Divine Mercy
An Imprint of Marian Press
2004

Nihil Obstat: Rev. Richard J. Drabik, MIC
Provincial Censor
January 1, 2003
(Solemnity of the Mother of God)

Imprimi Potest: Very Rev. Walter M. Dziordz, MIC
Superior of the Saint Stanislaus Kostka Province
January 1, 2003

Library of Congress Catalog Number: 2003100490

ISBN:0-944203-79-5

Typesetting: Patricia Menatti
Cover Design: Bill Sosa

Published by:
John Paul II Institute of Divine Mercy
An imprint of *Marian Press*
Marians of the Immaculate Conception
Stockbridge, Massachusetts 01262

Printed in the United States of America

For
Mr. Shaun Hillary, whose generosity and kindness has made possible the printing and publication of this — and many other books — on The Divine Mercy.

Table of Contents

Introduction

This book brings together reflections on the life and spirituality of St. Faustina by two priests who knew her personally as her spiritual directors, and by two others who devoted much of their lives to researching and extending her mission of mercy to the world. In that sense, this book enables the reader to get to know the great "apostle of Divine Mercy" through the minds and hearts of those who knew and know her best — a unique vantage point for understanding the heart of St. Faustina, and her spirituality of Divine Mercy.

Joseph Andrasz, S.J., was the priest who first provided Sr. Faustina with the wise and prudent direction she needed so that she could begin to cooperate with God's wonderful designs for her life. St. Faustina wrote of him in diary entry numbers 233-234:

His answers brought a great peace into my soul. His words were, are, and always will be **pillars of fire** which enlightened and will go on enlightening my soul in its pursuit of the greatest sanctity. ... From the moment the priest assured me that what I had experienced was not an illusion, but the grace of God, I have tried to be faithful to God in everything.

Fr. Andrasz became convinced of the holiness, and special mission given to St. Faustina, and in the years following her death, he became an ardent promoter of her message of Divine Mercy.

The Rev. Michael Sopocko, STD, was appointed to be the usual confessor to the convent of the Sisters of Our Lady of Mercy in Vilnius, where St. Faustina was stationed for several years. Our Lord spoke to the saint about him in these words: "This is My faithful servant; he will help you to fulfill My will here on earth" (diary entry 362). Indeed, Fr. Sopocko's spiritual direction became a great light upon her pathway, even though he was very exacting with her, and thoroughly tested the authenticity of her prophetic revelations from the Lord. No one was better placed than he was to know the essential elements of the Image of The Divine Mercy, as the Lord had revealed it to St. Faustina, and his reflections on this important subject, taken from his letters, are included in this volume.

The most in-depth theological analysis ever written on the life and mission of St. Faustina was provided for the Vatican in the 1970's by the *Rev. Ignacy Rozycki, STD,* a leading Polish Thomist, who also served as a member of The International Theological Commission for the Holy See. Fr. Rozycki devoted nearly a decade of his life to the task of making a thorough study of St. Faustina's *Diary*. The result of his labors was a tome of approximately 500 pages which was presented to the Vatican as part of the official investigation into Sr. Faustina's life and virtues by the Congregation for the Causes of Saints. We have provided in this volume the text of a lecture in which Fr. Rozycki beautifully summarized his research on the life and witness of St. Faustina.

The last portion of this collection was written by the *Rev. Seraphim Michalenko, MIC,* who has spent much of his priesthood researching and propagating St. Faustina's message of mercy. Fr. Michalenko served as one of the principal translators into English of St. Faustina's *Diary,* as vice-Postulator of the cause for her canonization, as Rector of the US National Shrine of The Divine Mercy in Stockbridge, Massachusetts, and as founding Director of the John Paul II Institute of Divine Mercy. In this volume Fr. Seraphim offers us a glimpse of the essence of St. Faustina's Way to holiness — a Way which divine grace began preparing for her from her earliest days as a devout little child of a devout Catholic family in the Polish countryside.

It has been my privilege to be able to work closely with Fr. Michalenko as his apprentice in Divine Mercy research, and to "carry the torch" for him, so to speak, as the second Director of the Institute. In the study of the Divine Mercy message, devotion, and spirituality, I truly "stand on the shoulders of giants." I am especially grateful, therefore, to Fr. Michalenko, and to the other three "giants" whose work is represented in this volume, for all that they accomplished for us, by divine grace, helping us all better to understand and appreciate the Merciful Love of God.

Robert Stackpole, STD

Director

John Paul II Institute of Divine Mercy

I.
Divine Mercy...
We Trust in You!

Written by:

Rev. Joseph Andrasz, S.J.

Translation edited by:

Rev. Seraphim Michalenko, M.I.C., S.T.L., S.E.O.L.

and

Robert Stackpole, STD

Introduction

Ever since the St. Stanislaus Kostka Province of the Congregation of Marians of the Immaculate Conception began to spread the devotion to The Divine Mercy in America in 1941, the community has received countless requests from people seeking more information on the revelations dealing with The Message of The Divine Mercy and on the life of Sister Faustina.

At first, the only information available on the Message was found in a little booklet entitled: "Novena to the Mercy of God," supplied by the Rev. Prof. Michael Sopocko, Sister Faustina's spiritual director.

In 1947, however, a pamphlet entitled: "Mercy of God... We Trust in You!" written by one of Sister Faustina's regular confessors, the Rev. Joseph Andrasz, S.J., of Cracow, arrived from Poland. It was translated and published within a year, and subsequently enjoyed many reprints.

The same author began to write a more extensive biography of Sister Faustina, but, for reasons reported here below, he was never able to complete it.

Saint Faustina's Diary contains a prophecy concerning the *work of mercy* (as Jesus called the whole complex of tasks He was entrusting to her). She wrote that this *work* will be, for a certain time, *as though utterly undone*, but that then *God will act with great power, which will give evidence of its authenticity. It will be a new splendor for the Church* (Diary, 378). Saint Faustina understood that this *work of mercy* was not something new, since it had been found in the Church from the beginning, although dormant for a long time.

The first part of this prophecy, "the undoing" of *the work*, was fulfilled in 1958, with a "decree" of condemnation by the Holy See. However, this severe ban was soon ordered by

Pope John XXIII to be mitigated, and four months later, in March 1959, it was replaced by a "Notification" of a disciplinary character in which, without any explicit condemnation, the Sacred Congregation of The Holy Office in Rome prohibited all spreading of devotion to the mercy of God *in the forms proposed by Sister Faustina Kowalska*. The "Notification" left a certain freedom of action to the discretion of Local Ordinaries with regard to the exposition of Images of The Most Merciful Savior for public veneration in churches.

As a direct result of this action, Fr. Andrasz's Superiors placed a moratorium on his biography of Saint Faustina and locked up the part he had already finished.

This prohibition of *the work of mercy* continued for twenty years. Fr. Andrasz died before it was lifted.

In 1967, the then Archbishop of Cracow, Karol Cardinal Wojtyla, successfully completed the first informative stage in the process for the beatification of the Servant of God Sister Faustina Kowalska. The outcome of the "Process of Information" showed that the action in Rome with regard to Sister Faustina was taken (at the least) on insufficient evidence. It must be remembered, however, that official communications between Rome and the Church in Poland during those post-war years, especially with regard to religious matters, were very difficult. Relevant, authentic documents could not be made available to the investigating authorities who were being pressed to make a judgment on the matter presented to them.

There exist several documents from the Holy See that show the history of the Church's position regarding the person of Saint Faustina and the message of which she was the instrument.

The first is the Decree of January 31, 1968, from the Sacred Congregation for the Causes of Saints by which her Process of Beatification was formally opened in Rome.

The second document deals with the message itself. The Sacred Congregation for the Doctrine of the Faith issued a "Notification" signed by the Prefect himself on April 15, 1978, which reversed the "Notification" of 1959.

Then, on July 12, 1979, an authoritative interpretation was given to the Superior General of the Congregation of Marians by the Prefect of the Sacred Congregation for the Doctrine of the Faith. In response to the request made in the name of the American Marian Province of St. Stanislaus Kostka for a clarification of the meaning of the "Notification" by which the former ban was rendered "no longer binding," Cardinal Seper wrote:

> ...I have the honor of informing [you] that with the new "Notification" (A.A.S., 30 June 1978, p. 350), arrived at in the light of original documentation examined also by the careful informative intervention of the then Archbishop of Cracow, Card. Karol Wojtyla, it was the intention of the Holy See to revoke the prohibition contained in the preceding "Notification" of 1959 (A.A.S., 1959, p. 271), in virtue of which it is understood that there no longer exists, on the part of this S. Congregation, any impediment to the spreading of the devotion to The Divine Mercy in the authentic forms proposed by the Religious Sister mentioned above [i.e., the Servant of God Sister Faustina Kowalska]. [NOTE: Our unofficial translation from the Italian.]

It is evident from this that Cardinal Wojtyla was instrumental in obtaining from the Holy See the complete reversal of its original decision regarding the devotion to The Divine Mercy.

The lifting of the ban on April 15, 1978, from the work of mercy proposed by Saint Faustina can be recognized as the beginning of the fulfillment of the second part of her prophecy. For, only six months after that event, a jubilant Church applauded Cardinal Wojtyla as the new Pope — John Paul II;

and within two years from that same event the Church received from this Pope and extraordinary encyclical entitled, *Rich in Mercy*. In it he set forth doctrinal and practical guidelines for a renewed understanding of, and recourse to, the God of Mercy in the Church.

Quite significant in this regard, also, was the visit this Pope made on the Feast of Christ the King, November 22, 1981, to the Shrine of Merciful Love in Collevalenza near Todi, Italy. There, within a few days, an international congress was to be held to reflect on the Encyclical *Dives in Misericordia* one year after its publication. It was the first time the Holy Father had traveled outside the City of Rome since his convalescence after the attempt on his life. There, after he had celebrated the Holy Sacrifice of the Eucharist, during his customary "Angelus Message", he made this public declaration:

> A year ago I published the encyclical *Dives in Misericordia*. This circumstance made me come to the Sanctuary of Merciful Love today. By my presence I wish to reconfirm, in a way, the message of that encyclical. I wish to read it again and deliver it again.

> Right from the beginning of my ministry in St. Peter's See in Rome, I considered this message my special task. Providence has assigned it to me in the present situation of man, the Church and the world. It could also be said that precisely this situation assigned that message to me as my task before God...

An official Decree was issued by the Sacred Congregation for the Causes of Saints on June 19, 1981, which declared that, with the required investigation of all the available writings of the Servant of God Sister Faustina Kowalska having been duly completed, there was nothing found in them to stand in the way of proceeding further with her Cause.

The Cause of Sister Faustina, therefore, began to move forward. On March 7, 1992, in the presence of the Holy Father, the Congregation for the Causes of Saints promulgated the Decree of Heroic Virtues, by which the Church acknowledges that Sister Faustina practiced all the Christian virtues to an heroic degree. As a result, she then received the title "Venerable" Servant of God.

Convincing evidence of miracles attributed to Sr. Faustina's intercession removed the last obstacle to the recognition of her sanctity by the Universal Church. And so, on the Sunday after Easter, Mercy Sunday, 1993, she was beatified by Pope John Paul II in St. Peter's Square in Rome, and then on Mercy Sunday, 2000, she became the first canonized saint of the new millennium. On these joyful occasions, the Holy Father spoke the following words, which sum up the significance of St. Faustina's life and witness for our troubled world:

"Her mission continues, and is yielding astonishing fruit. It is truly marvelous how her devotion to the merciful Jesus is spreading in our contemporary world, and gaining so many human hearts! This is undoubtedly a sign of the times — a sign of our 20th century. The balance of this century, which is now ending ... presents a deep restlessness and fear of the future. Where, if not in The Divine Mercy, can the world find refuge and the light of hope? Believers understand that perfectly ... What will the years ahead bring us? ... We are not given to know. ... But the light of Divine Mercy, which the Lord in a way wished to return to the world through Sr. Faustina's charism, will illumine the way for the men and women of the third millennium."

A Word About This Edition

In presenting this new edition of Father Andrasz's very popular booklet, we thought it appropriate to supply those sections of his original text that were not included in the original American publication. They were, for the greater part, addressed to readers in Poland, so, in 1948, the translators felt they were irrelevant to the American scene.

Since these sections contain eyewitness information on the early spread of the devotion, we felt they might be of interest. Thus, we decided, by means of this new edition, to present the author's work in its entirety.

It must be noted, too, that all passages quoted herein from the Diary of Saint Faustina Kowalska have had to be concorded with *the official, authentic text of that Diary* which was submitted to the Sacred Congregation for the Causes of Saints as an integral part of the canonical process for her beatification. Readers familiar with the former printings, therefore, should not be surprised to find some changes in the rendering of the texts.

The Polish edition of Saint Faustina Kowalska's writings, which were collected during the Process of Information toward her beatification, bears the *Imprimatur* of Franciszek Macharski, Metropolitan Archbishop of Cracow, Poland, dated April 18, 1979.

The endnotes for this edition were provided by the editors.

Fr. Seraphim Michalenko, M.I.C.

A WORD ABOUT THE AUTHOR

Father Joseph Andrasz, S.J., was born in Zakopane, Poland, on October 16, 1891. He entered the Society of Jesus on September 22, 1906, and was ordained a priest on March 19, 1919. Thereafter, he worked at the Jesuit Publishing House (*Wydawnictwo Apostolstwa Modlitwy*) for eight years. In 1930, Father Andrasz became the manager of the Publishing House and editor of the monthly magazine called "Messenger of the Sacred Heart" (*Poslaniec Serca Jezusowego*). From 1932, he was also the extraordinary confessor of the novices of the Congregation of the Sisters of Our Lady of Mercy in Łagiewniki near Cracow.

Sister Maria Faustina Kowalska went to confession to Father Andrasz in April, 1933, before making her final profession of vows. He was the first confessor to understand her and to set her completely at peace. He also advised her to pray for a spiritual director. Of him she wrote in her Diary:

> *Today I went to confession to Father Andrasz, this priest who is so filled with the spirit of God, who untied my wings so that I could soar to the highest summits. He reassured me in everything and told me to believe in Divine Providence. "Have confidence and go forward with courage." An extraordinary divine power came over me after that confession...* (Diary, 257).

On October 19, 1935, at the request of her spiritual director, Father Michael Sopocko, Sister Faustina consulted Father Andrasz concerning certain commands she had received from the Lord.

Also, it was Father Andrasz who at 4:00 P.M. on October 5, 1938, heard Sister Faustina's last confession. She died that night at 10:45 P.M.

Father Joseph Andrasz was in the process of writing a more extensive biography when a "Notification" from the Sacred

Congregation in Rome prohibited all spreading of devotion to the mercy of God *in the forms proposed by Sister Faustina Kowalska.* As a result, Fr. Andrasz's Superiors placed a moratorium on his biography. Fifteen years before the ban was lifted, Father Andrasz died on February 1, 1963.

Divine Mercy ... We Trust in You!

When the new devotion to The Divine Mercy — or rather, the old devotion to The Divine Mercy in a new form — was still in its embryonic stage, a leaflet entitled "Jesus, I Trust in You" was being circulated among the faithful. After the turmoil of the Second World War ended, this devotion made significant headway among our people, so that now, at the urgent request of many, we are bringing out this booklet entitled "Divine Mercy... We Trust in You."

I. GROWTH OF THE DEVOTION TO THE DIVINE MERCY

This devotion began to spread even before World War II, but quietly, in certain closed circles. The first time a fringe of this devotion made a public appearance was in 1935, in Vilnius, when the new *Image* of *The Divine Mercy* was placed in the Shrine of Our Lady of the Eastern Gate as part of the festal decorations on the occasion of the celebration of the closing of the Great Jubilee — the observance of the 1900th Anniversary of Redemption. It was during the three-day religious services marking the closing of the Jubilee Year that Father Sopocko, Sister Faustina's confessor in Vilnius, taken into confidence about this devotion at the Lord's command, delivered sermons on the immensity of the Mercy of God and on the Merciful God's desire that people turn to Him with great trust. Sister Faustina wrote that, while he was preaching, she was granted supernatural visions of the wondrous and generous way The Divine Mercy was acting in souls that were turning to Him with trust. For a long time after this event there prevailed a period of silence with regard to this devotion.

A second, more public action regarding this new devotion was the printing in Cracow in 1937 of a modest brochure. Its cover featured the new image of The Divine Mercy — based on the writings of Sister Faustina. This second action had a greater significance than the first. Through this brochure, printed, to be sure, with the permission of Church authorities, the new form of devotion to The Divine Mercy began to spread in a constant and ever-widening stream. It flowed out beyond private circles and slowly began to reach a wider public.

This took place while Sister Faustina was still alive. She was overjoyed to see how the devotion to The Divine Mercy in its new form was already capturing the hearts of people. However, except for a few persons who were taken into confidence, no one, not even those among whom she lived, knew that these prayers were composed by her under the special inspiration of God, as it is permitted us to believe.

During the War

Nevertheless, those actions were but hardly perceptible streams which began to swell only after Sister Faustina's death and, even more so, after the outbreak of the world war which she foretold. When the terrible wave of Nazism (1939-1945) descended with satanic brutality upon many nations, and especially upon Poland, the new devotion to The Divine Mercy began to grow with an even greater strength.

Printed and mimeographed leaflets containing information about the devotion, and about the saintly Sister Faustina to whom it was revealed, began to be circulated among the people, who eagerly took them up to read. As a result, not only did big cities like Warsaw and Cracow, Vilnius and Lvov, Poznan and Lodz become acquainted with the new images and medals of the Merciful Savior and with the litany and novena to The Divine Mercy, but the devotion also reached many smaller cities and village parishes. During the terrible oppression of war, people sought help by reciting the Chaplet to The Divine Mercy, or by trustingly wearing the medal, or by carrying the image of the Merciful Savior on their persons; and from many places came reports of wondrous and even miraculous answers to their entreaties. Not only did the devotion spread in Poland, but it also began to penetrate beyond its borders. Medals and holy cards of the Merciful Savior reached Polish troops in German prisoner-of -war camps, and civilian prisoners in concentration camps. They made their way to France and Hungary, to Romania and England, to Russia, Iraq, Palestine and Egypt — wherever a Polish exile was awaiting God's Mercy.

From eyewitnesses we know that this devotion was eagerly spread not only in Vilnius and its environs among the Poles, but also in the Kaunas region of Lithuania. The new images of The Divine Mercy, enshrined on small altars, were seen in the Cathedral of Kaunas and in many of the Lithuanian churches. Brochures containing the Novena, Litany and Chaplet to The Divine Mercy in the Polish and Lithuanian languages could be found at these shrines.

Polish displaced persons encountered the devotion in Bavaria, where it continues to flourish. It has been verified that this devotion is spreading in certain centers in the United States, Mexico, and even Australia.

After the War

But with the termination of the war, did not the fervor for this devotion also cease? For — as we say — "When in fear of the rod, we turn to God!" Certainly, some of the devotion's aspects, connected as they were with the urgent needs and immediate dangers brought on by the war, had ceased; but the devotion to The Divine Mercy itself in its new form is rather being strengthened and deepened, and it is making ever-widening circles. Post-war life is convincing the thinking public ever more deeply of the validity of the words that Jesus spoke to Sister Faustina:

Mankind will not have peace until it turns with trust to My mercy.

And whereas five to six years ago the image of the Merciful Savior was unknown in the churches, so presently [1947] these images are appearing in ever more of them; often they are of large dimensions, and artistically executed. One sees the faithful praying with confidence before them. Some of these images already have many votive offerings hung upon them by hearts grateful for relief in suffering, for conversion, for wondrous graces or outright miracles.[1]

In some churches, with the knowledge of the hierarchy, a monthly devotion is arranged for the faithful. Before the beautifully decorated Image of The Merciful Savior a priest celebrates Mass and preaches on The Divine Mercy; then all those present together sing the pensive litany to The Divine Mercy, and great numbers of the faithful receive Holy Communion.[2] Divine Providence so ordained that such solemn devotions to The Divine Mercy were first celebrated there where Sister Faustina gave back her beautiful soul into the hands of the Merciful Jesus. This place is Józefów, a convent of the Sisters of Our Lady of Mercy and an institution for the education and training of wayward girls. It is beautifully situated on a hill in Łagiewniki near Cracow (near the railroad station, Borek Fałęcki).

These devotions were begun during World War II, on March 7, 1943. Besides the local people, poor displaced persons who came from various parts of Poland and settled in this area until the end of the war, hastened in great numbers to participate in them. Later, the third Sunday of each month became the established day there for these devotions in addition to the first Sunday after Easter, which has come to be considered a kind of "Feast Day Indulgence" [in Polish — Odpust].[3]

Nor did these devotions stop when the war ended. They still keep drawing not only the local people but also a good number of "pilgrims" from Cracow itself.

After the devotions, held in Łagiewniki chapel, groups of the faithful often proceed to the convent cemetery where lie the

remains of Sister Faustina.[4] Through her intercession, they beg
for divine mercy for themselves and those dear to them. They
also commend to her intercession the fate of Poland, the
Fatherland so dearly loved by Sister Faustina.

II. RESERVATIONS CONCERNING THE DEVOTION

Looking at this somewhat rapid growth, one finds it difficult
to deny the impression that "the finger of God" is indeed here.

To be sure, with some people reservations arise: Why multi-
ply new devotions, new images and new practices? Are not the
existing ones more than enough? Others are fearful of illusions.
Indeed, before this new devotion, or rather this new form of it
(for the devotion to The Divine Mercy is as old as humanity
itself) receives final approval, it must undergo a very strict
examination. We do not wish to anticipate the final decree of
the Holy See as regards both, the devotion itself, and the wonderful, "miraculous" events in the life of Sister Faustina.

For a great number of followers of the devotion to The
Divine Mercy, precisely in this form, a principal support for it
— alongside other justifications — will be the opinion of the
experienced theologian Fr. Hyacinth Woroniecki, former
professor and rector of the Catholic University of Lublin. Not
too long ago there appeared in print his erudite study entitled
The Mystery of The Divine Mercy. In the Introduction, this is
what the author has to say about the devotion:

A Response to the Reservations

"On the eve of *the most difficult trial* that the Lord God
ordained to send upon our nation — having called us
almost ten centuries ago to His service, it pleased Him to
give us a special proof of His Mercy in order that we
would turn to Him with ever-increasing trust.

"For this purpose He enlisted the services of a lowly Polish girl, Helen Kowalska, in religion Sister Mary Faustina of the Congregation of the Sisters of Our Lady of Mercy who, having spent scarcely 33 years on this earth, passed on to a better life on October 5, 1938, leaving behind her the memory of one of those souls to whom God has granted the privilege of singular graces.

"The guiding thought of all the interior communications which she had received from Christ the Lord was *the mystery of God's mercy* and the obligation on our part to respond to it with a fullness of trust in Him.

"The beautiful image of the Lord Jesus — coming out, as it were, to meet us, and opening for us His bosom, from the depths of which the rays of His graces gush forth — is to make present to our senses the mystery of The Divine Mercy, of which Jesus is the eternal and perpetual personification; and the various prayers and invocations, which Sister M. Faustina composed under Divine inspiration, are to rouse souls to this unbounded trust for whose propagation in the midst of us all the saintly religious dedicated her life.

"The work, to which God called her, silent and hidden though it was during her lifetime, is beginning to grow more robust and to touch souls, fortifying them in times of most severe divine tests, which no one lacks in these times [following the war]. And no wonder, for we find in it nothing that would not gush forth *from the purest springs of Christian revelation*, that would not correspond to the *most orthodox traditions* of faith and Christian morality. We can, therefore, take to heart the appeals of Sister Faustina and give them a full response, *for everything in them reverberates with the authentic note of gospel teaching.*"

Truly, we would be hard-pressed for a more clearly expressed recognition and for finer praise.

III. THE PERSONALITY OF SISTER FAUSTINA

It is no wonder then, that so many have the great desire to learn something more about her whom the Savior Himself is said to have called to be a special confidante of His mercy, to whom He gave the commission to proclaim this devotion that is not only necessary for mankind, but, in the present times, is absolutely indispensable to it. We shall try to satisfy these valid desires fully somewhat later in a more comprehensive biography, in which we shall describe in greater detail the interior life of Sister Faustina, her relations with heaven, and her mission to be "the apostle of The Divine Mercy."

Exterior Personality

Helen Kowalska, known as Sister Maria Faustina in religion, was born in the village of Glogowiec, Poland, on August 25, 1905. At age 20 she entered the Congregation of the Sisters of Our Lady of Mercy (popularly known as the Magdalen Sisters), which devotes itself chiefly to the education and training of girls morally and financially impoverished. Accepted into the "second choir", she spent her postulant year [initial training] in Warsaw, and two years of novitiate in Łagiewniki near Cracow, where, too, she pronounced her first annual vows on April 30, 1928, and her perpetual vows — after five years — on May 1, 1933. She died five years later in Łagiewniki on October 5, 1938.

Religious obedience assigned her in turn to the various houses of her community in Warsaw, Plock, Walendow, Vilnius and Łagiewniki. There she worked for the most part in the kitchen, the garden, at housekeeping and gatekeeping. She labored diligently — like a worker bee; but also, like a bee, without publicity, quietly yet profitably. Besides the work, her life in the Congregation was filled out with prayer and, in a great measure, with sufferings — great ones at that.

The testimony of one of the older religious sisters gives evidence of how the life of Sister Faustina was perceived through the eyes of those who observed her at close quarters:

On the exterior, Sister Faustina did not distinguish herself by anything in particular, although, after our first conversation, I went away with the impression that this Sister was different from all the other Sisters. I admired her for her balanced spirit, her interior calm, and her cheerfulness of heart. I cannot recall that I was aware of any defect in her character. She was exemplary in the observance of the rule, in the performance of her duties, and in the fulfillment of her spiritual exercises. The tasks assigned to her were performed conscientiously and unsparingly so that everything would be in right order.

Interior Character

Such, more or less, was the external character of the life of Sister Faustina: grayish and unadorned, yet exemplary and edifying. Whoever had the opportunity, however, of getting to know Sister Faustina from the aspect of her interior life, and of delving into her spiritual Diary, written in strict obedience to her confessor, could not resist the strong impression that one was dealing with an uncommon soul. One saw in her a truly saintly servant of God who made rapid and lofty progress in Christian and religious virtues, and upon whom, at the same time, heaven lavishly bestowed its gifts and privileges.

Sister Faustina was well aware that the sanctity she fervently desired, and for which she entered religious life, did not depend primarily upon visions and revelations, but upon solid virtues. That is why even before she entered the religious life, but more especially while in the convent, she applied herself most earnestly to the acquisition of such virtues as purity of heart, humility, patience, conscientiousness, obedience, poverty, meekness, diligence, a charity ready to do kindness, interior recollection, deep devotion, and, above all, love of God.

One must not imagine that these virtues, especially in their high degree, came to her effortlessly. There is no doubt that she, too, committed little sins from time to time, whether it was in speech, or in her relations with others, or in certain reflexes that betrayed slight movements of impatience or vanity, or in some inexactness at work. She confessed them, sincerely begged God's pardon for them, but also energetically made every effort to overcome them. This she revealed in her Diary. Though from time to time she still succumbed to these little sins — for sanctity, even if heroic, is not yet, on this earth, the sanctity of heaven — nevertheless, there were progressively fewer and fewer of these infractions, and they became progressively smaller. On the other hand, lovely flowers of virtues unfolded ever more beautifully within her.

Virtues Recommended by The Blessed Mother

The Blessed Mother herself recommended to her the program for developing solid virtues within herself. "On the Feast of the Immaculate Conception," writes Sister Faustina, "I saw the Blessed Mother, inconceivably beautiful. Smiling at me she said to me:

> *My daughter, at God's command I am to be, in a special and exclusive way, your Mother; but I desire that you, too, in a special way, be My child. I desire, my dearly beloved daughter, that you practice the three virtues that are dearest to me, and most pleasing to God. The first is humility, humility, and once again, humility; the second virtue: purity; the third virtue: love of God. As My daughter, you must especially radiate with these virtues.*

When the conversation ended, She pressed me to Her Heart and disappeared. When I regained the use of my senses, my heart became wonderfully attracted to these virtues; and I practice them faithfully; they are as though engraved on my heart" (Diary, 1414, 1415).

Purity of Heart

We cannot treat fully within the covers of this small booklet all the virtues practiced by Sister Faustina, whose soul was adorned with them as a luxurious garden is adorned with flowers. Let us, however, say a few words about each of the three virtues particularly recommended to her by Our Blessed Mother.

As regards purity of heart, she wrote these words in her Diary just a year and a half before her death:

> God gave me the inner knowledge that I had never lost my innocence ... and that, in spite of all the dangers in which I had found myself, He Himself had been guarding me so that the virginity of my soul and heart would remain intact ... As often as I recall this inconceivable grace, that often a fresh flame of love and gratitude to God bursts forth from my heart ... I strive for the greatest purity of soul so that the rays of God's grace may be reflected therein in all their brilliance. I long to be a crystal in order to find favor in His eyes (Diary, 1095).

And she found it.

Humility

Sister Faustina applied herself untiringly and incessantly to the ever deeper cultivation of the virtue of humility, which is so pleasing to the Sacred Heart of Christ that He Himself tells us to learn it from Him (Mt 11: 29). She confessed that at times this cost her very dearly:

> As the soul continues to immerse itself more deeply into the abyss of its nothingness and need, God uses His omnipotence to exalt it. If there is a truly happy soul upon earth, it can only be a truly humble soul. At first, one's self-love suffers greatly on this account; but after a soul has struggled courageously, God grants it much light, by

which it sees how wretched and full of deception every-thing is ... O my Jesus, nothing is better for the soul than humiliations. In contempt is the secret of happiness ... And God, seeing the soul in such a disposition, pursues it with His graces (Diary, 593).

The one and the other was true in Sister Faustina's life: there was no lack of mortifying occasions — painful humiliations — which she bore courageously; but a hundredfold more numerous were the graces, extraordinary and magnificent ones, with which God pursued her, with which He sometimes overwhelmed her. This is the impression one often carries away upon reading her Diary.

Love of God

Saint Thomas teaches that Christian perfection is to be measured, above all, with the standard of charity, because love unites one with God, the ultimate goal of the human soul.

Sister Faustina possessed the virtue of the love of God to an eminent degree. There was found in her, first of all, that most essential proof of love of God which is doing God's holy will. Not only did Sister Faustina strive to fulfill God's holy will most perfectly, but she had a deep devotion to it.

During one very difficult trial she wrote:

My Jesus, You see that Your holy will is everything to me. It makes no difference to me what You do with me ... O will of God, You are the nourishment and delight of my soul! When I submit to the holy will of my God a deep peace floods my soul (Diary, 952). *Sweeter to me are the torments, sufferings, persecutions and all manner of adversities by divine will, than success, praise and esteem by my own will* (Diary, 678).

Her love for God was inflamed during her meditations and whenever she visited the Blessed Sacrament. How often her heart would take flight up toward God during her manual occupations! This love for God also became more deeply rooted in her by means of numerous trials and sufferings. The Holy Spirit inflamed Sister Faustina and embraced her soul with God's mysterious presence, which permeated her being through and through, even bestowing upon her heavenly visions — sublime ones at that! In confirmation of this action of the Holy Spirit, let us mention one of her heavenly visitations.

This particular one took place on the Feast of the Ascension in 1937.

Since early this morning, my soul has been touched by God. After I received Holy Communion I communed with the heavenly Father. My soul was drawn into the very glowing center of love. I understood that no exterior works could stand comparison with pure love of God ... I saw the joy of the Incarnate Word and I was immersed in the Divine Trinity. When I came to myself, longing filled my soul and I yearned to be united with God. Such tremendous love for the heavenly Father enveloped me that I call this day an uninterrupted ecstasy of love. The whole universe seemed to me like a tiny drop in comparison with God. There is no greater happiness than when God gives me to know interiorly that every beat of my heart is pleasing to Him, and when He shows me that He loves me in a special way (Diary, 1121).

From such an awareness of God, from such a going out on God's part, there arose in her soul an intense yearning:

O my Creator, l long for You ... All that is on earth seems to me like a pale shadow. It is You I long for and desire ... Oh, take me to Yourself, Lord! You know that I am dying, and I am dying of yearning for You; and yet, I cannot die ... Death, where are you? [Lord,] You draw me into the abyss of Your divinity, and You veil Yourself with darkness. My whole being is immersed in You, yet I desire to see You face to face. When will this come about for me? (Diary, 841)

At this point one could write a most beautiful chapter about Sister Faustina's keeping company with the inhabitants of Heaven. According to what she recorded in her Diary, she was very privileged in this regard. At times she had the happiness of keeping company with angels as did St. Stanislaus Kostka. The Infant Jesus often appeared to her, especially during Mass. She experienced, as though in the flesh, scenes from the Passion of Our Lord. She had many sublime revelations of the Most Holy Trinity. All this caused her not only to be penetrated by profound recollection, but also to be set on fire with the ardor of love and with an insuppressible yearning for God.

IV. SISTER FAUSTINA'S MISSION

But we must hasten to the most important matter of her life; for all these privileges, which will be the theme of a more elaborate exposition in a more extensive biography, were meant to prepare Sister Faustina for her great mission, namely, *to make known to the world the devotion to The Divine Mercy in its new form.*

All mankind, especially during this last century, is continuously straying farther and farther from God, from Christ, and from His Church. Consequently, in spite of the great progress of civilization, the world senses itself ever more disrupted and unhappy.

During this same century, in order to rescue erring and grievously sinful humanity, Heaven sent it extraordinary admonitions. It did this through Mary, the Mother of Mercy, who by means of three great apparitions — in La Salette, in Lourdes, in Fatima — exhorted humanity to penance and to a life based on faith and love. She made it clear that otherwise great calamities shall befall humanity for its unbelief and its immorality.

To the category of these revelations, whose purpose it is to turn back humanity from the path of godlessness, one must add the revelations given to Sister Faustina — given, this time, not in France or Portugal but in the land of graves and crosses that is our Poland. It is the Savior Himself who appears in these revelations as the chief personage, who with the new revelation of His mercy wants to convert sinful humanity, to draw it away from the paths of destruction; for, as He had often stated with emphasis to His confidante:

Mankind will not have peace until it turns with trust to My mercy (Diary, 300)

Revelation of The Divine Mercy

Sister Faustina received the *first apparition* of Jesus as *The Merciful One* on February 22, 1931, in Plock. She described it thus:

In the evening, when I was in my cell, I saw the Lord Jesus clothed in a white garment. One hand [was] raised in the gesture of blessing, the other was touching the garment at the breast. From beneath the garment slightly drawn aside at the breast there were emanating two large rays, one red, the other pale.[5]

In silence I kept my gaze fixed on the Lord; my soul was struck with awe but also with great joy. After a while Jesus said to me:

Paint an image according to the pattern you see with the inscription: Jesus, I trust in You. I desire that this image be venerated first in your chapel and [then] **throughout the world** (Diary, 47).

Along with this instruction of Our Lord, Sister Faustina noted two promises given by the Savior:

I promise that the soul that will venerate this image will not perish. I also promise victory over [its] enemies already here on earth, especially at the hour of death. I Myself will defend it as My own glory (Diary, 48).

Sister Faustina received, then, an unusual vision of the Savior, because it was a representation of Him which hitherto she had never seen. Then again, she received a command to paint an image of a new content. This was truly a burdensome order for a simple religious sister who was knowledgeable in domestic matters, but to whom matters of art and painting were totally foreign.

The Meaning of the Image

The vision of the Merciful Jesus in this particular representation. occurred repeatedly during Sister Faustina's lifetime. Our Savior evidently wanted the image to be deeply impressed upon her soul. Before the first image of this kind was painted, however, many hardships and unpleasant experiences lay in store for the Sister. Today there exist many images after this type. Let us explain their symbolic meaning.

First of all, what is the meaning of the two great rays, red and the pale, shining forth from the bosom of Jesus — those rays by means of which, from now on, all people will immediately recognize that they have before them an image of The Divine Mercy?

When, at the request of her confessor, Sister Faustina asked the Lord about this matter, she received, while at prayer, this clarification:

The two rays denote Blood and Water — the pale ray stands for the Water which makes souls righteous; the red ray stands for the Blood which is the life of souls. These two rays issued forth from the depths of

My most tender mercy when My agonized heart was opened by a lance on the cross. These rays shield the soul from the wrath of My Father. Happy is the one who will dwell in their shelter, for the just hand of God shall not lay hold of him[6] (Diary, 299).

During His Passion our Savior shed almost all of His Precious Blood for us. Some of It remained in His dying Heart, so He permitted that a lance should open this Most Sacred Heart; then the Blood gushed forth from It to the last drop, and Water with it. The Savior wants this touching manifestation of His Love to be venerated in a special manner in the devotion to The Divine Mercy. It is for this reason that He instructed Sister Faustina to write down this short ejaculatory prayer and to use it often:

O Blood and Water, which gushed forth from the Heart of Jesus as a fount of mercy for us, I trust in You[7] (Diary, 186, 187, 309).

Though these two rays represent the most characteristic mark of the image of The Divine Mercy, other details within it, in their own way, likewise underline the mercy by means of which Jesus wants to attract souls to Himself. And thus, the Savior represented in this image is not riding on clouds as a Lord and Judge, but is *walking upon this our poor earth,*[8] upon whose inhabitants He wants to bestow His Mercy.

Both the hands of Jesus also serve the idea of mercy. The left hand points to the bosom, to the Heart — namely, to *the source* of mercy; it ushers us into His very "heart of hearts". The right hand, moreover, the Savior raises on high[9] — not to threaten and punish, but to bless yet more lavishly from now on those who will have recourse to His mercy.

And what are we to say of the *white garment* without a cloak? — for that is the way Our Lord appeared to Sister Faustina. Is it to be a symbol of purity of heart which mankind, infected by godlessness and contaminated by immorality, needs so badly? It may be so, and the interpretation is plausible. But a different thought comes to mind. Doctors and nurses attending the sick put on white garments as a sign that they are ready to serve and to heal. And so, the Lord's white tunic can be a symbol of His great readiness to heal ailing humanity by means of His mercy.[10]

In the expression of the face and eyes of the Savior there should shine through the fatherly seriousness that sadly beholds erring humanity; but there should also shine through the fatherly Love that takes pity on it and is ready to gather it to Its Merciful Heart.

So that no one should be uncertain as to what sentiments this image is to inspire in souls, it should bear the inscription, **Jesus, I Trust in You**. Our Lord was speaking of just such an image when He said to Sister Faustina:

> **I am offering people a vessel with which they are to keep coming for graces to the fountain of mercy. That vessel is this image with the signature: "Jesus, I trust in You"** (Diary, 327).

Trust

Trust! — *That is the great cry of Jesus in this devotion.* Just as by means of the devotion to His Most Sacred Heart He wanted to awaken in us sentiments of mutual love, especially expiatory love, so once again, by means of this devotion, He desires to enkindle in our wayward hearts sentiments of the deepest possible trust — quite simply, a limitless trust — in His mercy. The Savior cried:

> **The flames of mercy are demanding that I spend them; I want to keep pouring them out upon souls...** (Diary, 1074).

He sorrowfully complained about distrust:

Distrust on the part of souls is tearing at My heart of hearts. The distrust of a chosen soul causes Me even greater pain; despite My inexhaustible love for them, they distrust Me... (Diary, 50).

He commanded Sister Faustina to write for the consolation of all people:

Let the greatest sinners place their hope in My mercy. They have the right before others to trust in the bottomless depth of My mercy... They give Me great pleasure — those souls that make an appeal to My mercy! To such souls I grant graces surpassing their desires. I cannot punish even the greatest sinner if he makes an appeal to My compassion, but, on the contrary, I justify him in My unfathomable and inscrutable mercy...(Diary, 1146).

The Savior keenly exhorts people to hasten to Mercy before Justice closes in:

Write: before I come as a just Judge, I first open wide the door of My mercy. He who refuses to pass through the door of My mercy must pass through the door of My justice[11] (Diary, 1146).

By means of visions, our Lord often gave Sister Faustina to understand the enormity of humanity's sins. Horrified by their hideousness, she asked Him how He could suffer such gross insults. His reply:

I have eternity for punishing [these]**, and so I am prolonging the time of mercy for the sake of** [sinners]**. But woe to them if they do not recognize the time of My visitation... Secretary of My mercy, your duty is not only to write about and proclaim My mercy, but obtain grace for them with your entreaties, that they, too, may glorify My mercy** (Diary, 1160).

At another time Jesus said to her:

Write that the greater the misery of a soul, the greater its right to My mercy; [urge] all souls to trust in the unfathomable abyss of My mercy, because I want to save them all. On the cross, the fountain of My mercy was opened wide by the lance for all souls — no one have I excluded! (Diary, 1182).

V. MEANS TO ATTAIN THE GOAL

One who sincerely wants to attain a goal, especially a great one, must use the proper means to attain it; otherwise, one runs the risk of being justly criticized for entertaining a fleeting fancy instead of acting upon a genuine desire. Hence, Our Redeemer *wants*, indeed, it is His *ardent desire*, that presently there be stirred up in humanity a new surge — a new conversion, by means of which it will be saved.

On what will this conversion depend? It will depend on people's willingness to recognize and admit that they erred grievously: that they broke off from the source of their peace and happiness because they turned away from God and from Christ. And it will next depend upon this, that they acknowledge their misfortune and their sin. But they will not be able to do that unless they are drawn, by the knowledge of God's inexhaustible mercy, to seek help with great confidence and trust.[12]

Our Savior, then, coming again with a message of mercy, is only calling our attention anew to that basic condition — which we know under the name of repentance — that alone is capable of rescuing humanity at every moment, but especially now, from the turmoil which is capable of plunging the world into a catastrophe greater than the one we experienced not so long ago [World War II]. The following words spoken by the Savior to Sister Faustina should ring loudly and continually in our minds:

Mankind will not have peace until it turns with trust to My mercy (Diary, 300).

In order to evoke this conversion to The Divine Mercy in individual hearts as well as in entire nations, the Savior offers a variety of means. The devotion to The Divine Mercy must be, above all, internal; but since human beings are not only spirit but also body, their inner devotion must have its *external expression* and its *external means*.

The Image of The Divine Mercy

The *first* of these external means, and at the same time a most expressive symbol of the entire devotion to The Divine Mercy in its new form, is the *image of the Merciful Savior*. Its characteristic representation is meant to evoke, in the minds of all who look upon it, a vivid notion of the inexhaustible Mercy of God, and to elicit in hearts a profound confidence in Jesus, who is its personification.

And this representation of the Merciful Savior — as paintings, prints and medals which already have been circulated by the hundreds of thousands — is, indeed, continually spreading its salutary message wherever it goes.[13]

The Feast of Mercy

However, Our Savior wants to evoke this widespread and powerful turning-again to His Mercy not only from individual souls, or even families, but from humanity in general. That is why He offers another external means, which by its universality, is to reach wide masses of people. To this end, through His confidante, He is demanding the establishment of a new feast:

I desire that the first Sunday after Easter be celebrated as the Feast of Mercy (Diary, 49, 299).

The history of the Catholic Church demonstrates that there are a number of feasts towards the establishment of which private revelations were instrumental or helpful. Among these are: the Feast of The Body and Blood of Christ (Corpus Christi), introduced as a result of the revelations received by Blessed Julianna of Cornillon; the Feast of The Most Sacred Heart of Jesus, influenced by the revelations given to St. Margaret Mary Alacoque; as well as the Feast of Christ the King. From among the feasts of Our Blessed Mother we mention the Feast of Our Lady of Mt. Carmel, of Our Lady of Lourdes, and the Feast of The Immaculate Heart of Mary, which was promulgated throughout the Catholic World by Pope Pius XII as a result of the revelations of Our Blessed Mother in Fatima, Portugal.

We see, therefore, that the influence of private revelations on the establishment of new feasts in the Catholic Church is not something altogether new.[14] It is to be understood, however, that, besides this, every feast must find its deep basis in Public Revelation [the Sacred Scriptures and Tradition].

Our Savior wants this feast to play a very important part in the context of the new form of devotion to The Divine Mercy. That is why He attaches great graces and privileges to this feast. Let us read what Jesus said about this to Sister Faustina.

My daughter, tell the whole world about My inconceivable mercy. I desire that the Feast of Mercy be a refuge and shelter for all souls, and especially for poor sinners. The very depths of My tender mercy are opened on that day. I pour out a whole ocean of graces upon those souls who will approach the fount of My mercy. The soul that will go to Confession and receive Holy Communion shall obtain complete forgiveness of sins and punishment ... Let no soul fear to draw near to Me, even though its sins be as scarlet ... This Feast emerged from the very depths of My mercy and it is confirmed in the vast depths of My tender mercies ...

I desire that it be celebrated with great solemnity on the first Sunday after Easter (Diary, 699).

It is clear from the above that: firstly, Jesus earnestly desires the establishment of this feast; secondly, that, just as for the feast of His Heart He designated a certain determined date, namely, the Friday after the Octave of Corpus Christi, so too, for the Feast of Mercy He also designated a specified date: it is to be the first Sunday after Easter.[15] Finally, He attaches to this feast an unusually generous outpouring of graces upon souls who on that day will run to His Mercy with confidence.

It may take some time before the Church will institute the Feast of The Divine Mercy. In the meantime, however, we may observe it privately.[16]

Worshipers of The Divine Mercy should keep this in mind, however, that before the Feast of Corpus Christi was introduced, and especially the Feast of the Heart of Jesus, it was necessary to overcome many difficulties. This can likewise be the case concerning the feast in honor of The Divine Mercy. They should, therefore, be prepared for this, that Divine Providence will require from them great pains and effort, and especially fervent prayers, before the highest Church authorities assent to the establishment of the new feast.

For such is the supernatural law, that the greater the glory that a certain work is to give to God, and the greater the good that is to come to mankind because of it, *that* many more problems and difficulties does Satan, and human spite and apathy as well, set up against it. Consequently, those who love this work must develop an even greater energy, foresight and zeal.

The Chaplet of The Divine Mercy

In the writings of Sister Faustina we find still other means which may serve to spread and to deepen our devotion to The Divine Mercy. Two of these, which, according to Sister

Faustina, were revealed to her and imposed upon her by The Savior Himself, merit our special attention. The first is the "Chaplet" and the second is the "Novena to The Divine Mercy". Both of these devout practices are already widely known and used.

The revelation of the *Chaplet to The Divine Mercy* occurred in the midst of some moving and even terrifying moments. On September 13, 1935 (Diary, 474), Sister Faustina was caught up in a vision in which she beheld an Angel, who was the executor of divine wrath, with bolts of thunder and lightning flashes in his hands. At the sight of this sign of divine wrath, which was to come upon the earth, and especially upon a particular place, she began to implore the Angel for mercy. She had the feeling, however, that in the face of divine wrath her prayer was a mere nothing.

Just then she beheld the Holy Trinity. She was overwhelmed by Its majesty and incomprehensible holiness. Simultaneously, she heard within herself words by means of which, with extraordinary power, she began to beg help for the world. And imagine! In the face of this prayer the Angel became helpless and unable to carry out the just punishment. These were the words with which she was entreating God:

Eternal Father, I offer you the Body and Blood, Soul and Divinity of Your Dearly Beloved Son, Our Lord Jesus Christ, for our sins and those of the whole world. For the sake of His sorrowful Passion, have mercy on us and on the whole world (Diary, 475).

The following day, on entering the chapel, she heard within her these instructions:

Every time you enter the chapel, immediately recite the prayer I taught you yesterday.

As soon as she did what she was told, within her she heard these words:

This prayer will serve to appease My wrath.[17] You will recite it for nine days on an ordinary pair of rosary beads in the following manner:

First of all, you will say one OUR FATHER, one HAIL MARY, and the I BELIEVE IN GOD.

Then, on the OUR FATHER BEADS you will say the following words:

"Eternal Father, I offer You the Body and Blood, Soul and Divinity of Your dearly beloved Son, Our Lord Jesus Christ, in atonement for our sins and those of the whole world."

On the HAIL MARY BEADS you will say the following words:

"For the sake of His sorrowful Passion have mercy on us and on the whole world."

In conclusion, THREE TIMES you will recite these words:

"Holy God, Holy Mighty One, Holy Immortal One, have mercy on us and on the whole world." (Diary, 476)

Such was the origin of the Chaplet to The Divine Mercy. It teaches us many things: namely, 1) that human malice brings down divine punishment upon the world;[18] 2) that heavenly spirits take part in the carrying out of these punishments; and this, 3) that the entreaties of a saintly soul exert a great influence in warding off divine chastisement if that soul appeals to Jesus Christ, to His Passion.

It is our Lord's desire that by means of this chaplet we frequently render worship to Him as The Divine Mercy, and with our entreaties obtain mercy for ourselves. Just how pleasing this devout practice is to Our Lord is attested to by the promises He made known through Sister Faustina:

Oh what great graces I will grant to souls who will recite this chaplet! Write down these words, My daughter. Speak to the world about My mercy; let all mankind recognize My unfathomable mercy. It is a sign for the end times; after it will come the day of justice (Diary, 848).

At another time Jesus said to His servant:

Continually keep on reciting that chaplet which I have taught you... My mercy will embrace during their lifetime, and especially in the hour of death, those who will recite the Chaplet ... Priests will be offering it to sinners as the last security when all else has failed ... I desire that the whole world know about My mercy. I desire to give unimaginable graces to those who trust in My mercy (Diary, 687).

Sister Faustina herself came to be convinced of the great efficacy of this Chaplet to The Divine Mercy on a number of occasions, but especially whenever she applied it for the souls in Purgatory, and, even more so, when she recited it for the benefit of those who were experiencing great sufferings while in their last agony. Let us, too, become convinced of its efficacy.

Novena to The Divine Mercy

Entering somewhat yet more deeply into the devotion to this same Divine Mercy is the *Novena to The Divine Mercy*. It is to be joined by a more intimate bond to the Feast of The Divine Mercy itself, for Sister Faustina entitled its entry in her Diary thus: *A Novena to The Divine Mercy which Jesus instructed me to write down and to make before the Feast of Mercy. It begins on Good Friday* (Diary, 1209).

Our Lord also gave her instructions about what she was to do on each day of this Novena. These activities are worthy of the Most Merciful Heart of The Savior and extremely beneficial to us:

1) I desire that during these nine days you bring souls to the fount of My mercy, that they may draw therefrom strength and refreshment, and whatever graces they have need of in the hardships of life, and especially at the hour of death.

2) On each day you will bring to My Heart a different group of souls and you will immerse them in this ocean of My mercy ... You will do this in this life and in the next ...

3) On each day you will beg My Father, on the strength of My bitter Passion, for graces for these souls (Diary, 1209).

Let us take note of the words: *You will do this ... in the next life.* It becomes evident from them that Jesus wants to make of Sister Faustina an intercessor with The Divine Mercy not only in this life, but also in eternity. He also promised that her intercession will have extraordinary efficacy.

Sister Faustina said to the Savior in all simplicity, *Jesus, I do not know how to make this novena and which souls to bring first to Your Most Compassionate Heart* (Diary, 1209). Then Our Lord instructed her to bring all mankind on the first day, especially sinners — on the second day, the souls of priests and religious — on the third, the devout and faithful — on the fourth, those who do not believe in Him and those who do not yet know Him — on the fifth, separated Christians: **they tore at My Body and Heart, that is, My Church** — on the sixth, the humble and meek, as well as the souls of little children — on the seventh, the souls who especially venerate and glorify His mercy ... **These souls will shine with a special brightness in the next life** — on the eighth, the souls detained in Purgatory — on the ninth day, the lukewarm souls: **My soul suffered the most dreadful loathing in the Garden of Olives because of lukewarm souls ... For them the last security when all else has failed is to take refuge in My mercy** (Diary, 1210 to 1229).

Sister Faustina was to immerse each of these groups in the boundless sea of Christ's mercy and thus to bring them into contact with the benefits of His Saving Passion.

The Novena to The Divine Mercy composed by Sister Faustina can be made at any time; but, according to Our Lord's wishes, the dates fixed for its celebration are from Good Friday to the First Sunday after Easter.

Jesus, wrote Sister Faustina, *is commanding me to make a Novena before the Feast of Mercy, and today* [on Good Friday] *I am to begin it for the conversion of the whole world and that Divine Mercy come to be known* (Diary, 1059).

[Jesus elaborated on these intentions by explaining:]

... so that every soul will praise My goodness, I desire trust from My creatures ...Let the weak, sinful soul have no fear to approach Me, for even if it had more sins than there are grains of sand in the world, all will be drowned in the immeasurable depths of My mercy (Diary, 1059).

On the Feast of The Divine Mercy (April 4, 1937), which followed upon the conclusion of this Novena, Sister Faustina's soul was immersed in the depths of the Divinity and in a mysterious way it was united with the Three Persons of the Most Blessed Trinity:

My soul was flooded with joy beyond understanding and the Lord gave me to experience the whole ocean and abyss of His fathomless mercy. Oh, if only souls would want to understand how much God loves them! All comparisons, even if they were the most tender and the most vehement, are but a mere shadow when set against the reality (Diary, 1073).

We see, therefore, how pleasing this Novena to The Divine Mercy is to the Savior. We cannot demand, in truth, that our novenas be crowned with extraordinary outpourings of graces of the kind received by her whom the Lord had chosen to be the "secretary and apostle" (Diary, 965, 1142, 1273, 1588) of His mercy; there is no doubt, however, that this Novena, celebrated with fervor, and above all, with great trust, will be a powerful means of obtaining for ourselves and for others an abundance of divine gifts.[19]

VI. OTHER AIDS

Are there other means of stirring up — not only in individual souls, but in all mankind as well — a profound devotion to The Divine Mercy, other than the four enumerated above: namely, 1) the Image of The Divine Mercy; 2) the Feast of Mercy; 3) the Chaplet; and 4) the Novena to The Divine Mercy? No doubt these four will always remain singularly important, for according to the testimony of Sister Faustina, they were prescribed by the Savior Himself.[20]

In her spiritual Diary, however, we do find still other means as, for example, *her own prayers* to The Divine Mercy which burst forth from her heart like fiery sparks capable of inflaming in other hearts a lively devotion to The Divine Mercy. On the basis of one of these prayers there already was composed a Litany to The Divine Mercy which is widely known and is being sung during services in various centers. Sister Faustina's prayers, full of praises for The Divine Mercy, enlivened with great trust, often, too, with apostolic zeal, when published as a separate collection, most certainly will set afire similar sentiments in other hearts as do presently the aforementioned Litany, Novena and Chaplet.

A powerful means for evoking in souls a widespread and deep turning to The Divine Mercy will undoubtedly be a more extensive biography of Sister Faustina. It is only a more complete work that will be able to reveal to what heights of virtue the Savior called her; how deeply He allowed her to partake of His sufferings; to what degree He permeated her with the spirit of His mercy. Only a more complete biography will reveal the great wealth of extraordinary, heavenly graces and mystical gifts with which God was pleased to enrich the soul of this humble and unknown religious sister. And He did all that in order to prepare her to be a worthy **secretary and apostle of** [His] **mercy**, as He was pleased to call her on several occasions.

By means of this modest booklet, our primary aim was not to bring Sister Faustina to the fore, but rather those things that would enable a wider audience to become better acquainted with the devotion to The Divine Mercy in its new form, and to gain deeper understanding of it. However, according to the loving designs of the Savior, the very person of the saintly Sister Faustina is to play a special role in the spreading of the devotion to The Divine Mercy. The Lord wishes to make her a special intermediary and advocate in this matter. Sister Faustina herself was clearly aware of this mission, that she will be drawing souls to The Divine Mercy not only during her short earthly life, but above all in eternity, for she wrote:

> *I am perfectly aware that my mission does not end with death, but will begin. O doubting souls, I will draw aside for you the veils of Heaven to convince you of God's goodness, so that you would no longer continue to wound with your distrust the Sweetest Heart of Jesus. God is Love and Mercy* (Diary, 281).

For this reason, a comprehensive biography of Sister Faustina becomes in a certain sense a necessity.

Challenges and Promises

The human heart is capable of attaining selflessness; but in this human heart there are so many desires — even very lofty ones — and at the same time there is so much helplessness, that it eagerly looks around for someone who would willingly come to its aid. Our Savior is well aware of these two peculiarities of the human heart. That is why time and again He appeals to the most noble selflessness. More often, however, to provoke us to action, He appeals to the human heart with a promise of help. This is exactly what He does to encourage us to spread the devotion to The Divine Mercy in our own hearts as well as in the hearts of our neighbors.

Jesus is well aware of the spiritual poverty of every soul, of the great misery of humanity today. He knows that except by turning to The Divine Mercy, neither the individual soul nor mankind will be healed. At the same time, His Most Sacred Heart is so filled to overflowing with this mercy that He suffers torment when He cannot pour out its healing streams upon human hearts — and He cannot, because they do not turn to mercy for them; they do not want to accept it.

That is why from the Savior's Heart, which is "patient and of great mercy", which at all costs desires to save, come to us through Sister Faustina these lamentations and challenges:

My daughter ... the flames of mercy are demanding that I spend them; I want to pour them out upon people's souls. Oh, what pain they cause Me when they are not willing to accept them! Proclaim, My daughter, that I am Love and Mercy Itself ... Do whatever is within your power to spread devotion to My mercy. I will make up for what you lack ... (Diary, 1074). **Speak to the world about My mercy. Let all mankind recognize My unfathomable mercy. It is a sign for the end times; after it will come the day of justice. While there is still time, let them have recourse to the fount of My mercy ...** (Diary, 848). **Let the sinner be not afraid to approach Me** (Diary, 50, 1059).

I desire that priests preach this great mercy of Mine towards sinful souls (Diary, 50).

These are challenges; and there are many of them scattered throughout the pages of Sister Faustina's Diary. Along with them go many precious promises of the Lord for those who venerate The Divine Mercy and for those who spread this devotion:

I promise that the soul that will venerate this image [of The Divine Mercy] **will not perish. I also promise victory over** [its] **enemies already here on earth, especially at the hour of death. I Myself will defend it as My own glory** (Diary, 48).

These rays [red and pale, symbolizing the Blood and Water that gushed forth from the Sacred Heart] **shield souls from My Father's wrath... Happy is the one who will dwell in their shelter, for the just hand of God shall not lay hold of him** (Diary, 299).

The souls who spread the honor of My mercy I shield through their entire life as a tender mother her infant, and at the hour of death I will not be a Judge for them, but the merciful Savior. At the last hour a soul has nothing with which to defend itself except My mercy. Happy is the soul that during its lifetime immersed itself in the Fountain of Mercy, because justice will have no hold on it[21] (Diary, 1075).

We stated that the Merciful Savior is well aware of the great misery of mankind today — of the material misery, but even more particularly of the moral misery. Through this humble sister, Jesus is appealing to humanity, first of all, by means of a warning — that it will exert itself fruitlessly if it does not have recourse to The Divine Mercy. Let us hear again how this solemn warning sounds:

Mankind will not have peace until it turns with trust to My mercy (Diary, 300).

The Savior does not content Himself with giving a warning, but turns to an erring humanity with a cordial appeal and a joyful promise:

Tell aching mankind to snuggle close to My merciful Heart, and I will fill them with peace (Diary, 1074).

Whoever knew the simple and unlearned Sister Faustina had no doubt that, of herself, she would not have been capable of making up this warning and appeal that have such a far-reaching scope and such great importance. Here someone infinitely greater than she is speaking — someone who has the right to warn all of mankind and at the same time to lovingly invite it to come back to Him, and to promise it, in return, the good which it so ardently desires: **I will fill them with peace.**

The Merciful Heart of Sister Faustina

Speaking of "other aids" that widely and strongly are to attract souls to Jesus' Mercy, one should find it difficult not to mention, even briefly, what role Sister Faustina's merciful heart is to play in all this. The Savior wanted the future "Apostle of His Mercy" to form her sentiments and her whole conduct in accordance with this great attribute. In her life we find many instances which give witness to how thoroughly imbued she was with this desire of the Lord Jesus, so that we can rightly speak of "the merciful heart of Sister Faustina".

First of all, she exercised mercy towards the poor through material help according to the means of the convent. And she did this so enthusiastically and heartily that the Savior manifested to her in a miraculous way how pleasing to Him were those little works of mercy.

Moreover, the Lord drew her heart yet more strongly toward those works of mercy which bring not only temporal relief but which, by their effects, have a bearing on all eternity. It was a matter of helping sinners, the dying, and the souls in

Purgatory. This triple devotion kept developing continually in Sister Faustina's soul. Here, in corroboration of the above, are a few examples:

About ten thousand people die each hour, and many of these pass away after a very sinful life without spiritual ministration. These unfortunate persons find themselves in danger of eternal damnation. Is it not the greatest work of mercy to save these souls? *I often attend upon the dying,* wrote Sister Faustina, *and through entreaties I obtain for them trust in God's Mercy ... God's mercy sometimes touches the sinner at the last moment in a wondrous and mysterious way ... the soul, illumined by a ray of God's powerful final grace, turns to God in the last moment with such a power of love that in an instant it receives from God forgiveness of sin and punishment ... Oh, how beyond comprehension is God's mercy!* (Diary, 1698)

I am often in contact with persons who are dying (Diary, 1684), wrote Sister Faustina. It was her Guardian Angel (Diary, 820) who would prompt her to do this. It often happened that the persons dying were several hundred kilometers away. *A wondrous contact with the dying has God given me! My vision is purely spiritual, by means of a sudden light that God grants me at that moment. I keep on praying until I feel peace in my soul* (Diary, 835). More than once she was able to ascertain that indeed it was at this juncture, when she was summoned to prayer, that the final agony of the given person was beginning. She likewise ascertained that whenever she was compelled to pray for a longer period of time, it meant that that soul was undergoing greater struggles and was experiencing a longer period of agony. She became convinced that the Chaplet to The Divine Mercy was especially helpful to the dying.

Recite the chaplet I have taught you (Diary, 810), said the voice she heard within her soul on one such occasion; and she felt the power of The Divine Mercy embrace the dying person.

Out of a fervent desire to save the dying from eternal damnation, the merciful heart of Sister Faustina grew bold in its petitions. She recalled, for example, that on a Friday, January 8, 1937, during Holy Mass, she felt the closeness of the Lord in a special way. After Holy Communion she turned her gaze with trust toward the Lord and began to entreat Him thus:

O Jesus! I beg You by the inconceivable power of Your mercy that all the souls that will die today escape the fire of hell, even had they been the greatest sinners. Today is Friday, the memorial of Your bitter agony on the Cross. Because Your mercy is inconceivable, the Angels will not be surprised at this (Diary, 873) ...

And the Lord pressed her to His heart and said:

My beloved daughter, you have come to know well the depths of My mercy. Know that you have requested a great thing from Me, but I see that this was dictated by your pure love for Me; that is why I am complying with your requests (Diary, 873).

For the *souls in Purgatory*, too, Sister Faustina had a heart full of compassion and of readiness to help. Knowing well that they no longer are able to help themselves in their excruciating suffering, she frequently interceded for them to The Divine Mercy, offering her prayers and sufferings for them. God permitted the suffering souls to clearly commend their needs to her and even to let her know of the relief of bliss granted to them.

And finally, *sinners* — their conversion was her great concern. Jesus wanted her to have a heart as compassionate as His own, that she be *inflamed with Mercy*:

Today [March 25, 1938] *I saw the suffering Lord Jesus. He leaned down toward me and whispered softly:* **My daughter, help me to save sinners.**

Suddenly, a burning desire to save souls entered my soul. When I recovered my senses, I became aware by what means I was to help souls and I prepared myself for greater sufferings. Today my suffering increased, in addition, I felt wounds in my hands, feet and side … I sensed the hostility of the enemy of souls, but he did not touch me (Diary, 1645, 1646).

Sister Faustina knew how to intercede for a multitude of sinners not only through suffering, but also through prayer so admirably full of most wonderful simplicity and compelling confidence. Does not the prayerful conversation with the Lord quoted here below remind us of the plea, famous for its trustfulness, which Abraham made for Sodom and Gomorrha?

This morning [February 16, 1937] *after completing my spiritual exercises, I began at once to crochet. I sensed a silence in my heart, I sensed that Jesus was resting in it. That deep and sweet consciousness of God's presence prompted me to say to the Lord: O Most Holy Trinity, dwelling in my heart, I beg You: Grant the grace of conversion to as many souls as the* [number of] *stitches that I will make with this crochet hook today.*

Then I heard these words in my soul: **My daughter, too great are your demands!**

Jesus, you know that for You it is easier to grant much rather than a little.

That is so … But every conversion of a sinful soul demands sacrifice.

Well, Jesus, I offer You this whole-hearted work of mine.

This offering does not seem to me to be too small for such a large number of souls; after all, Jesus, for thirty years you were saving souls by just this kind of work; and since holy obedience forbids me to perform great penances and mortifications, therefore, I ask You, Lord: Accept these mere nothings stamped with the seal of obedience as great things.

Then I heard a voice in my soul: **My dear daughter, I comply with your request** (Diary, 961).

These wondrous incidents can be considered as having been a preparation for the important message that Our Lord was to give Sister Faustina four months before her death.

It was the beginning of June, 1938. She was lying gravely ill in one of the sanatoriums in Cracow, commonly referred to as "Prądnik". Along with the sufferings, God bestowed upon her numerous graces. Among them was this one, which one might call "The Testament of Mercy". Once again the Savior impressed upon her the greatness of His Mercy:

Know, My daughter, that My heart is Mercy Itself. From this sea of mercy graces flow out upon the whole world. No soul that has approached Me has ever gone away unconsoled. All misery gets buried in the depths of My mercy, and every saving and sanctifying grace flows from this fountain (Diary, 1777).

Having stated to His servant in so solemn a manner the power of His mercy, the Savior declared what she is to be, by His most gracious will, with regard to this mercy:

My daughter, I desire that your heart be an abiding place of My mercy. I desire that this mercy flow out upon the whole world through your heart. Let no one who approaches you go away without that trust in My mercy which I so ardently desire from souls (Diary, 1777).

These great and splendid statements of Jesus, which, in our opinion, assign to the humble Sister Faustina an immensely extensive mission, demand some clarification. This we will present in a more comprehensive biography. For the time being, let what has been written here inspire a deep trust in the efficacy of the intercession of the new "secretary and apostle" of Jesus' mercy. For, private devotion to saintly servants of God, even though they have not yet been "beatified", is not only permitted, but is in accord with the mind of the Church.[22]

VII. THE BLESSED MOTHER AND THE NEW DEVOTION

It is always an important matter for the Catholic heart to know whether or not there exists any relationship between the Most Blessed Mother and a given cause; and, if there does, to recognize the nature of that relationship. For, if one is evident, we grow to an effectively stronger conviction concerning that cause.

Well, then, Sister Faustina, on several occasions, was honored with a vision of the Blessed Virgin. We shall mention here only the vision of March 25, 1936. It exhibits much of the great importance of our Lady's apparitions at La Salette, Lourdes, and lately in Fatima,[23] and, it would seem, even surpasses them in this respect. Indeed, besides the importance, it can be said that the vision is pervaded with a certain gravity.

On that particular day of Our Lady's Annunciation, an especially deep feeling of the presence of God swept over Sister Faustina during her morning meditation. She saw the infinite greatness of God and at the same time His inexpressible condescension towards creatures in the Mystery of the Incarnation, which came to pass precisely on the day of the Annunciation. Then Our Blessed Mother appeared to her. First of all, She expressed Her praise for souls who faithfully follow the inspirations of divine grace. Then She addressed to Sister Faustina words, which, on the one hand, convey exceeding honor for her, while, on the other hand, they show forth the unparalleled importance of the devotion to The Divine Mercy on the present age.

Let us give our attention to what Our Lady said further to the one whom Her Son chose for an apostle of The Divine Mercy:

I gave the Savior to the world; as for you, you have to speak to the world about His great mercy and prepare the world for the Second Coming of Him, who will come, not as a merciful Savior, but as a just Judge. Oh how terrible is that day! Determined is the Day of Justice, the day of divine wrath. The Angels tremble before it. Speak to souls about this great mercy while it is still the time for [granting] *mercy. If you keep silent now, you will be answering for a great number of souls on that terrible day. Fear nothing. Be faithful to the end. I sympathize with you* (Diary, 635).

VIII. OUR OBLIGATION

If Our Blessed Mother, that "kind-hearted" Mother who loves us all so very much, speaks in this manner, what conclusion must we draw from it? Only this, that it is not a third-rate matter with which we are dealing, but a cause that is of vital concern for us. Therefore, as regards the Devotion to The Divine Mercy in its new form, we cannot be indifferent or negligent, as though the matter left us neither hot nor cold. On the contrary, when Heaven stands before us with such a splendid gift, we should understand that it is our duty to do our very best, our utmost, to root and ground this devotion in our own hearts first. Are we already doing this?

Next, we should understand that we ought to propagate it prudently, but at the same time earnestly, in our own social circles, and especially among those who have gone astray, for they are in greatest need of The Divine Mercy. We should all do our part in this regard by a variety of means so that our entire country become inflamed with this devotion.

Finally, let us make the above our great and holy ambition, so that the blessings of Jesus connected with this devotion to The Divine Mercy might flow through us upon all of mankind.

We gather from her Diary that Sister Faustina dearly loved her country: *O Poland, my dear homeland!* she exclaimed at one point, *If you only knew how many prayers and sacrifices I offer to God for you!* (Diary, 1083) As a matter of fact, she prayed much and did penance for Poland's benefit, at times directly at Heaven's command. She also had certain enlightenments with regard to Poland's destiny.

The last words which Sister Faustina wrote about her beloved Poland, more or less four months before her death, have a certain mysterious aspect about them. They are pervaded with great hope, and they seem to connect the destiny of Poland with this "work of Mercy".

She wrote: *While praying for Poland, I heard these words:*

I have grown particularly fond of Poland, and if she will be obedient to My will, I will exalt her in might and holiness. From her will come forth the spark that will prepare the world for My final coming (Diary, 1732).

At the beginning of this booklet we saw that The Devotion to The Divine Mercy in its new form had spread here and there, beyond the borders of Poland, into other countries.[24] In the main, however, up to now, it has been growing mostly in Poland, particularly in certain centers there. [Editor's Note: Let us bear in mind that this was written in 1947. Since then, the situation has changed greatly.] This is not surprising. After all, it was in Poland that the devotion was born, before so dreadful a catastrophe at that. It pleased the Savior to call one of Poland's peasant girls to great sanctity and to choose her to be the "apostle and secretary of The Divine Mercy".

However, she has already gone back to the Lord. She was but the initiator of this great and profound movement which is to lead the straying world back to The Divine Mercy. Most certainly she will be interceding with God for this great cause. As a matter of fact, after one of her lengthier conversations with the Savior, at the end of which He assured her that by reciting the Chaplet she was bringing mankind closer to Him, she uttered this fervent prayer:

> *O my Jesus, though I will go to You and You will fill me with Yourself, nevertheless I will not forget about humanity. I desire to draw aside the veils of heaven, so that the earth would have no doubts about The Divine Mercy ... O how ardently I desire that all mankind turn with trust to Your Mercy* (Diary, 930).

Upon us, then, the living worshipers of The Divine Mercy, rests this great and privileged task of seeing to it that this devotion encompasses ever new hearts, ever new localities in our country, so that no one and no place would remain untouched by it.

The next task awaiting us is to see to it that this age-old devotion in its new form conquers other lands and peoples — indeed, the whole of humanity. Some, and perhaps many, may say, "This goes beyond our strength!" We answer, "Ours — yes! But if we join our little strength to that of Jesus, to whom 'is given all power in heaven and on earth'; and if we *trust without bounds*, as our Lord demands from those who worship The Divine Mercy; surely, we will be able to perform this gigantic but also splendid task."

Mankind must energetically and completely shake off a double falsehood in which a notable part of it has been enmeshed for the longest time: the first falsehood — as though mankind were not dependent upon its Creator and His laws; the second falsehood — as though before Him mankind were not guilty of sins, and grave ones at that. The recognition of its essential dependence upon God, and acknowledgment of its great sin, which is apostasy from the Creator and His laws, from Christ and His Church — these two are only the first, yet necessary, conditions for mankind to be able to turn effectively to the sources of its salvation.

The one who points to these sources is mankind's Redeemer — He, who called Himself the Son of Man — Jesus Christ. He solemnly proclaims that, for this present age, *the inexhaustible springs of divine mercy* are the source of salvation for the human race and that it is to these that humanity must turn wholeheartedly.

It is we, the worshipers of The Divine Mercy, who must cry out to the whole world so strongly, that mankind will take heed and understand the serious warning coming from the best of its Sons, Jesus Christ, Himself:

Mankind will not have peace until it turns with trust to My mercy (Diary, 300).

At the same time, it is from us that there must ascend to heaven powerful cries and fervent petitions for this purpose: that, having paid heed to this grave warning, mankind might, with all its strength, respond to the fatherly appeal of its Savior, who, through one of its own daughters, pleadingly offers this invitation:

Tell aching mankind to snuggle close to My merciful Heart and I will fill them with peace (Diary, 1074).

Most certainly, the Savior will fulfill His promise — I will fill them with peace — provided that the aching human race carries out the condition set before it.

Let us fervently pray for this! Let us not cease in our endeavors and efforts, for a great deal is at stake! Let us do this with IMMENSE TRUST!

Endnotes for Divine Mercy... We Trust in You!

1.   Not only are Images of The Divine Mercy appearing in ever more churches in Poland, but at least one of the new churches in almost every diocese in Poland today bears the patronal title of "The Divine Mercy."

2.   In the Church of St. Florian in Warsaw, for example, ever since concelebration was restored in the Latin Rite, a large number of priests concelebrate at the monthly Divine Mercy celebrations held there, usually with a bishop as the principal celebrant, and quite often with several bishops participating. The same happens at a number of other centers of the Devotion.

3.   Since 1980 these devotions are held at Jozefow on the *third Friday of each month* for the following reason:

Upon his first visit to his homeland, Pope John Paul II requested of his countrymen that they, particularly, back his pontificate with their prayers. In response, special services for his intentions are held in most churches throughout Poland on the day closest to the 16th of the month — the date in October, 1978, on which the first Pole ever was elected to become the Pope of Rome. In many places, apart from the Holy Eucharist, it is prayers to The Divine Mercy that are specially offered up for him; in the first place the Chaplet. After 1980, when it was approved for use in Poland, the Votive mass of The Mercy of God is also widely celebrated on this occasion whenever the liturgical rubrics allow it.

4.   On November 25, 1966, during the Process of Information in preparation for her beatification, the remains of the Servant of God Sister Faustina were exhumed and laid to rest within the Sisters' chapel in Łagiewniki in a separate tomb located beneath the floor near the wall to the right of the main entrance. Later, her remains were transferred to a tomb on a side altar, beneath an Image of The Divine Mercy.

5.   ... in the sense of "colorless" or "clear".

6.   The expressions "... the *wrath* of My Father" and "... the *just hand* of God ... lay hold of him" might strike the reader as being completely out of place within the context of a message dealing with "God's mercy". They must, therefore, be understood correctly. In the Scriptures, human feelings, actions, and physical parts are often attributed to God, not that they are really in Him, but because such effects proceed from Him, much as the effects that flow from such things in our human experience.

The *wrath of God*, far from being the effect of a mood-swing in God, is *a state in the human being* which results from one's deliberate turning from a God who has revealed Himself in the created universe (see Rm 1: 18-23). Divine anger is essentially *the human being's self-imposed alienation* from a Good God, and the results of this separating of one's self from one's source are moral chaos and perversion of the moral conscience (see Rm 1: 23-32).

Therefore, the statement "Christ's Blood and Water shield the soul from *God's wrath*" expresses the fact that the soul is actually protected from *the evil consequences* (the rotten fruits which are the natural effects of sin) which the soul *has invited upon itself* when it cut itself off by sin from God's ever-flowing and divine-life-giving as well as divine-life-preserving blessings.

As long as *we cling* to sin, we can experience God only as *wrath*, for *we do not permit ourselves* to take advantage of God's forbearance in order to escape the punishment which God wants to withhold from us: "Wrath and anger are hateful things, yet the sinner hugs them tight" (Sir 27: 30). When that is the case, because of the resulting perversion that affects our moral conscience, instead of acknowledging: "I'm to blame for my hurtful situation" (being struck by the lightning attracted by the lightning-rod that I refuse to let go), we shift the blame, exclaiming: "God is angry with me!"

When we realize, further, that the Scriptural image of "Blood and Water" (which gushed forth from the Savior's side when it was pierced on the Cross) stands for Christ's *voluntary offering of His own life* by which He became "the propitiation [the sacrifice that atones] for our sins..." (1 Jn 2: 2), this symbol of the "shielding rays" expresses the truth that, when we turn to Jesus with *trustful acceptance* of the forgiveness He won for us, He is the One who, by taking away sin, *turns aside from us the hurtful consequences* that we brought upon ourselves by our sin (see Rom 3: 24-26).

7.   Perhaps Our Lord's calling our attention to His Blood surprises us, as does also the use of blood in the sacrifices of the Old Covenant and the insistence of the Hebrews on blood throughout the holy scriptures. We have to remember, then, that, according to the expressions used in the Bible, *blood is life*: "Since the life of a body is in its blood, I have made you put it on the altar, so that atonement may thereby be made for your own lives, because it is the blood, as the seat of life, that makes atonement" (Lev 17: 21).

Therefore, according to the Old Testament principle (re-stated in the Epistle to the Hebrews, namely: "... without shedding of blood there is no redemption" — 9: 22), it was not the creature designated for sacrifice that constituted the offering for sin (for, when slain, it was nothing more than a cadaver), but it was the "warm blood", or the "live blood", that is, the victim's life, which had to be "poured out". Otherwise, the sacrifice was null and void — that is, it had no effect towards forgiveness of sin or towards re-instating a normal relationship with God that was broken by the human being.

If we accustom ourselves mentally to substitute the term "blood" with the expression "life offered", many texts of sacred scripture, instead of seeming strange to us or even repugnant, could become awesomely evocative.

The sacrifice of blood, then, embodied the meaning of "offering one's life" in obedience to God, trusting that He has our best interests at heart. That obedience is the surest sign of "devotion", that "solid attachment" to our loving Creator-Father, that enables us to enjoy the inheritance He made possible for His creatures to share in union with His Only-begotten Son.

8.   The booklet here presented in translation was one of the earliest popular pieces of literature to have been published on Sister Faustina and her mission. It was this statement made by Fr. Andrasz in the booklet that influenced various artists to paint their versions of the Merciful Christ of Sister Faustina's vision as *walking upon this our poor earth*, and so with a background of fields, hills, trees and flowers — a background that is totally absent from the original image of The Divine Mercy that was painted under Sister Faustina's *personal direction.* (See the "Appendix" to this essay below.)

9.   This "soaring" expression of the author likewise influenced artists to paint Christ's arm in the image of The Divine Mercy as *raised high*, which is contrary to Sister Faustina's repeated insistence. This is attested to by her spiritual director, one of the very few persons to have heard the Sister give the directives to the artist, whom he himself found and commissioned to paint the original image. Fr. Sopocko claims that Sister Faustina insisted that the right hand, raised in blessing, should be depicted as not exceeding the height of the Lord's shoulder (see the "Appendix" to this essay.)

10.   This interpretation, interesting as it might be, cannot compare with the rich meaning that the white tunic evokes when seen from the point of view of the Bible against the background of texts like Leviticus 16: 23-24; Ezekiel 44: 18; John 19: 23b; Revelation 1: 13 — all of which point to the conclusion that the person so clothed is the Great High Priest of the New Covenant who, by His voluntary sacrifice of self for His beloved creatures,

assures those under the covenant the most important thing every human being wants to be assured of: "... I will forgive their wickedness and will remember their sins no more" (see Epistle to the Hebrews 3: 1-6; 4: 14; 5: 10; and Chapters 7-10).

11. It should be understood that our Lord is using the word *justice* here in the meaning that people *most commonly* give to that word, and which theologians define more precisely as "vindictive" justice, that is, justice that demands punishment, or reparation, for wrongdoing. This form of divine justice will be experienced *only by those* who will persist, even in the last moment of their earthly life, in a conscious and firm decision *not to accept God's merciful love.*

St. Paul assures us that there is in the Scriptures another, more basic, idea of "justice" — understood as an essential characteristic of God — which he defines as *God's faithfulness to His promises*, which He made to all who will believe in Him and trust in Him (see Rm 1: 17). This positive concept of justice is simply another face of mercy. It is, therefore, not something to be dreaded.

12. See Pope John Paul II's Encyclical, *"Dives in Misericordia"* — "conversion to God always consists *in discovering His Mercy,* that is, in discovering that love which is patient and kind as only the Creator and Father can be; the love to which the 'God and Father of our Lord Jesus Christ' is faithful to the uttermost consequences of the history of His covenant with man: even to the cross and to the death and resurrection of the Son. Conversion to God is always the fruit of the 'rediscovering' of this Father who is rich in mercy" (VII, 13, par.6).

13. In some earlier pieces of literature dealing with the Message of The Divine Mercy and with the devotion connected with it, there is a particular promise mentioned, alleged to have been attached by Our Lord to the Image of The Divine Mercy, namely:

When punishments for sins shall come upon the earth, and your native land shall be in extreme abasement, the only salvation will be hope in Divine Mercy. I shall preserve the cities and homes in which this picture shall be found; I shall protect likewise those persons who shall venerate and have confidence in My Mercy (*Novena to The Mercy of God*; Author not indicated, Congregation of Marian Fathers, Stockbridge, Mass. and Detroit, Mich., 1944, p. 32. Also, in similar words, in *Devotion To Divine Mercy In Our Day,* Fr. Julian Chrosciechowski, M.I.C., Congregation of Marians, Stockbridge, Mass. & London, Engl., 1976, pp. 27-28).

IT MUST BE DECLARED HERE that, although this statement, attributed to Our Lord, *may have* actually been transmitted by Sister Faustina during her lifetime to her spiritual director (who appears to be the source of our knowledge of it), the words quoted herein above are *nowhere to be found in the official collection of Sister Faustina's existing writings.* Therefore, until their true source and authenticity can be uncovered and verified, they cannot be vouched for as being authentic.

At the same time, however, it must also be stated that very many persons have attested to the fact that they acted upon that alleged promise with trusting faith, and have experienced as a result nothing less than outrightly "miraculous" protection in dangerous, grave or hopeless situations. (See letters on file with the Congregation of Marians, Stockbridge, Mass.)

14.   In connection with the fact that "private revelations" do play an important role in directing the Church's actions — proof of which can be found throughout Her history — it is heartening to realize that in recent years theologians have come to grips with the need of adjusting their stance with regard to "private revelations".

In general we content ourselves with a distinction between the one "Public Revelation", that of the Gospel, and the many "private revelations", lumping together in the second category all the supernatural communications made to the "mystics". We usually add that only the first is of obligation, the second, at the most, being allowed to be accepted and held as true with a purely human faith, that is, resting on human testimony.

For several years now, however, certain theologians have felt obliged to make distinctions between, on the one hand, those supernatural communications whose immediate object is the good and the management of the souls of those to whom they are made, and, on the other hand, those made to the recipients to be communicated by them to the whole Church. And they arrive at the conviction that, *from the moment it is established that God is speaking to us, by Himself or by a messenger, His word justifies an act of faith which belongs in a certain manner to the supernatural order*. God's word is the basis of it and demands it; there is an obligation to believe and therefore to obey. For it is a question, these theologians tell us, of prophecy.

In very forceful words St. Paul clearly stated: "The Church is built upon the foundation of the apostles and prophets" (Eph. 2: 30), meaning the prophets of the New Testament, as is shown beyond the shadow of doubt in the context. He also stated: "Extinguish not the Spirit. Despise not prophesies. Hold fast that which is good" (Thess. 5: 19-20). Saying: "Hold fast", St. Paul is here giving an order.

That is why St. Thomas Aquinas himself went as far as to say that "Prophecy is necessary for the government of the people and [*he adds in an emphatic way*] principally on what concerns divine worship, for which nature is not adequate: grace is necessary." Following St. Augustine, St. Thomas affirmed also that "there was never a lack of men possessing the spirit of prophecy, not to propose new doctrine of faith *but to direct man in his actions," "so far as that was necessary for the salvation of the elect.."* That necessity would have no meaning if it did not include the obligation to believe in prophecy.

The theologians concerned assert, therefore, that the repeated invitation of the Second Vatican Council to respect charisms should open minds today to that theology of *prophetic charism* and to its essential function in the divine economy of the government of the Church. So, then, they assure us that, when the Popes consecrate the world to the Heart of Christ or to the Heart of Mary [or, we could add, establish a new Feast in the Church] at a request made to them by the prophetic route and after satisfying themselves that their action fits perfectly the requirements of the New Covenant — discernment of the charism presented to them having been duly exercised — the step they take is not just legitimate; it is the response to a duty of the supernatural order which is obligatory.

The Message of Mercy, proclaimed by St. Faustina Kowalska, for which the way had been prepared in the Church by a long line of "mystics" (some of whom have also been declared Saints), appears to be what the Holy Spirit is indicating to the Church as a means "necessary for the salvation of the elect" today, in the light of the theological conclusions here related. Our Lord's "demand" for a Feast — by which His Mercy will be duly honored and sinners will be attracted to relinquish their sin and return with utter trust to the arms of their loving Father — does not appear to be a light matter at all.

With her beatification and canonization, the revelations St. Faustina received from Our Lord with a solemn message to the Church and the world have to be taken into consideration as seriously as those granted to St. Margaret Mary Alacoque (concerning the Sacred Heart of Jesus), to Bernadette Soubirous (the Lourdes message), and to the children at Fatima, not to mention others, which the Church eventually acted upon in a solemn way.

15.   The reader should be aware of the fact that in the Roman Missal and liturgical books, after the Liturgical reform of Vatican Council II, the *first* Sunday *after* Easter is officially called " The *Second* Sunday *of* Easter".

16.   From several entries in Sister Faustina's Diary it is clear that *Our Lord considered the "Feast of Mercy"* which He wants celebrated solemnly in the Church on the first Sunday after Easter, to be actually existing. Our Lord's words referring to this matter were recorded in her Diary (88). There He is quoted as having said plainly: **That Sunday is the Feast of Mercy**.

On another occasion, when Sister Faustina was offering her prayers, work and sufferings to Our Lord so that the Feast of Mercy be established in the Church, she said to Him:

But, Jesus, I have one word to say to You: I am very surprised that You bid me to speak about this Feast of Mercy, for they tell me that there already is such a feast; and so why should I speak about it? And Jesus said to me: **And who knows anything about this feast? No one! Even those who should be proclaiming My mercy and teaching people about it often do not know about it themselves** (Diary, 341).

In another entry, Jesus is quoted as saying:

My Heart rejoices on account of this Feast (Diary, 998).

17.   See Footnote 6 on the way to understand the expression: "divine wrath".

18.   An eminent scholar of Sacred Scripture, Fr. George Montague, S.M., gives us a good explanation of how we are to understand statements about "God's punishment". He states: "In the biblical view, sin is its own punishment and the evil God brings on sinners is primarily allowing their own schemes to bear their rotten fruits" (*Building Christ's Body*, p. 88).

St. Paul assures us of God's never-changing intent by insisting that God gave Jesus up to be a sacrifice of atonement for us, that is, as the one who would turn aside the wrath (the hurtful result which is present wherever sin comes in) by taking away sin.

19.   With regard to the Novena that Our Lord wants us to make before the Feast of The Divine Mercy, we should take special note of something else that Sister Faustina wrote in her Diary:

> *The Lord told me to recite this chaplet for the nine days before the Feast of Mercy. It is to begin on Good Friday. Then He told me*: **By this novena, I will grant every possible grace to souls** (Diary, 796).

From this and other passages in the Diary, it appears that the Lord wants us to make novenas *of the Chaplet* for whatever need.

With most people devoted to The Divine Mercy, the novena of prayers described by Fr. Andrasz has taken precedence over the Novena of Chaplets to which Our Lord attached such a sweeping promise for anyone who prays it.

Perhaps they do not sufficiently realize that the promise Our Lord attached to the novena for which He dictated the intentions applied to Sister Faustina alone, for He said to her on that occasion:

> **I will deny nothing to any soul whom you** [singular] **will bring to the fount of My mercy ...** (Diary, 1209).

Anyone making a novena to The Divine Mercy, therefore, should seriously consider including the Chaplet of Mercy as part of it.

20.   Fr. Andrasz appears not to have considered a few other elements that, with those he mentioned, are presented in Sister Faustina's Diary as together constituting the devotion to The Divine Mercy indicated by the Lord Himself, namely: 1) The remembrance of His Passion at 3 o'clock in the afternoon if only for a very short moment; 2) Frequent recourse to the Sacrament of Reconciliation, but especially in connection with the Feast of Mercy; 3) The proclamation of (announcing of, making known publicly) the Divine Mercy so as to stir up trust in people towards God; and 4) Above all, the reception and

worshiping of Jesus in the Most Holy Eucharist — the very source of Mercy Itself on earth.

21.   See footnote 18 above.

22.   Early in her Diary (Notebook I, p. 13), in all simplicity, the Saint recorded a vision she was given about her own exaltation by the Lord. She saw herself hurrying towards the altar of the convent chapel from where a voice was telling her to take her place on the altar, while everyone around her was throwing at her whatever they could get their hands on, so that she was forced to make her way quickly to the designated spot on the altar. The great crowd included her superiors, fellow sisters, the girls the sisters took care of, and even her parents. As soon as she got to the designated place on the altar, however, the people who made up that same crowd began to stretch forth their hands and beg for graces. And the Sister added that she didn't hold it against them that they were throwing all those things at her, but that in reality she felt a more particular love precisely for those persons who thus forced her to advance more quickly to the place designated for her. At that moment inconceivable happiness flooded her soul and she heard these words:

Do as you will, hand out graces as you will, to whom you will and when you will (Diary, 31).

Instantly the vision vanished.

23.   It must be kept in mind that even at the time this booklet was written (1947), very little was known in Poland and elsewhere around the world concerning the happenings in Fatima in 1917.

24.   In the second edition of Fr. Andrasz's work, bearing the imprimatur of His Eminence Prince Adam Stefan Cardinal Sapieha, he includes the following information.

Vatican radio aired a program on February 24, 1948, entitled, "Sister Faustina, an apostle of Divine Mercy." The program stated:

The Lord Jesus found delight in [Sr. Faustina's] soul, and chose her for an apostle of His mercy, instructing her to rouse sinners to repentance and trust in His mercy, especially in times of harrowing trials which have, or which will fall on our country and on humanity.

Fr. Andrasz also tells of a letter he received from the United States, informing him of the spread of the message and devotion in that country. Fr. Andrasz writes:

The devotion to the Divine mercy in its new forms is spreading beyond the borders of our country, and a telling example of this is a letter which the author of this booklet [Fr. Andrasz] received from the United States, from Eden Hill, Stockbridge, Massachusetts, from Fr. Joseph Sielski, MIC, dated November, 1947. It contains the following information.

"Here in America this devotion is spreading at a fast pace. Our Congregation [The Congregation of Marians of the Immaculate Conception] is also involved in its spread. We began this work after the arrival of one of our priests from Russia. He brought with him a description of the revelations of Sr. Faustina, and a "pro memoria" of Fr. Sopocko. First it was the Felician Sisters who became interested and published the Novena to The Divine Mercy in the Polish language. Soon after we were also encouraged to do the same. To this day, we have published the Novena (the Chaplet, Litany, and brief description of this new devotion) in both the Polish and the English languages. We have published 50,000 Novenas in Polish, 100,000 in English, and 250,000 Images. We have also prepared for publication the Novena together with the Chaplet and a description of the revelations in the French language. The "pro memoria" of Fr. Sopocko was reprinted, and we have mailed it to all of the ordinaries of the United States and Canada, and also to the rectors and presidents of seminaries and universities. We could do much more, however, if we had more people for this work. We have opened up a special office for the promotion of the Divine Mercy message. Every year before the Feast of Mercy we mail a circular letter to the names on our files encouraging them privately to recite the Novena and to receive Holy Communion on the first Sunday after Easter."

Finally, Fr. Andrasz tells of the initial steps taken by the hierarchy towards the approval of the devotion by the Holy See:

The favorable attitude of the whole Polish episcopate to the cause of the Divine Mercy in its new form is to be considered the most significant amont the preparatory steps. This favorable attitude was expressed not only by the quiet aquiescence to its spread in our own country, but above all by this fact: that our bishops, at one of their plenary meetings, decided to present this matter to the Apostolic See, together with the request for the institution of the Feast of The Divine Mercy on the first Sunday after Easter. As we know from the lips of His Eminence the Primate [Cardinal Hlond], the Congregation of Sacred Rites is already considering this matter. The Theological Society, at its convention in Cracow in April of 1948, resolved to direct a similar petition to the Holy Father.

Appendix

Rev. Michael Sopocko concerning the Image of The Divine Mercy

I.

(Written to Dr. Julian Chrosciechowski, later a Marian Father, on April 29, 1949.)

Regarding the description of the image, according to Sister Faustina, the image is to represent the Lord Jesus in a walking posture, clothed in a long white garment with a band [belt] round the waist. The eyes must be somewhat cast down, and the look [gaze], as from the cross, merciful. With the right hand he's to be blessing the world, and with the left, opening [drawing aside] the garment in the area of the Heart. From under the open [drawn aside] garment there are to be gushing [streaming, bursting] forth two rays: on the right of the onlooker a pale [= colorless] one, and on the left a red one. These rays are to be transparent, but appropriately throwing light on the figure of the Savior, as well as on the area [space] in front of Him.

II.

(Written to Fr. Julian Chrosciechowski, MIC from Bialystok on April 1, 1956.)

We should base the devotion to The Divine Mercy upon public revelation whose expression is the liturgy of Low Sunday [now officially: the Second Sunday of Easter]. Circles [agents] exercising deciding control over such matters have immense reservations about private revelations (thanks to certain Sisters of the Congregation of Our Lady of Mercy) and in the year 1953 forbade the introduction of the Divine

Mercy Image into churches, as coming from a private unverified revelation. Only after separating this devotion from
private revelations and basing it on the Gospel and liturgy
was it possible to obtain a recommendation for all pastors of
souls in the country to solemnly observe Low Sunday with
worship of God in His Mercy, which pours itself out upon the
world in the sacrament of baptism and penance. This
occurred thanks to an article entitled "The Spirit of the
Liturgy of Low Sunday," a copy of which I'm sending along
with this letter and which I authorize you to publish.

The image is also to come from public revelation (John 20,
19 ff). That's why I had to provide a background of the doors
of the Cenacle (which besides is consonant with Sister
Faustina's thought [mind]). Copies of this image that you asked
for I enclose herewith, as also of the Kazimirowski prototype,
which is the most correct one. Were someone to paint, he ought
to take the prototype as his model, for the new image by
Slendzinski is likewise not the ideal one, nor is the Łagiewniki
one [ideal]). In this first one [painting] of Slendzinski there is
still a lot of "feminism" (the right hand is too far away from the
body, the head is unnecessarily inclined, the right foot catches
too much attention and the rays are too faint [indistinct, weak]).

The Hyla image must have been painted in 1946, since I
already found it in 1947 and I ascertained the following deficiencies: blatant feminism, the whole figure is curved (as
though dancing); the right hand raised too high, expressing
action (drama or comedy), and not composure [serenity]; the
rays overly materialistic, like ropes; a skittish look directed
somewhere into space; an inappropriate background (formerly
there were flowers, and now a tile floor and the blue of the sky
— no logic).

The image should represent Christ at the moment of instituting the sacrament of penance with the words "Peace to you!":
the right hand at the height of the shoulder, the eyes directed

downward; the whole figure frontally expresses and bestows peace; the rays should be directed towards the onlooker, and not towards the ground. The background [should be] dark or [there should be the] doors of the Cenacle. The image is to be the visual commentary of the liturgy of Low Sunday: "I saw water..." "Three there are that give witness..." (the reading), the institution of the sacrament of penance [reconciliation] (the gospel). ...

III.

(A letter to the same Rev. Father Julian from Bialystok dated September 18, 1956, re-emphasizes:)

Please take as the pattern for the new image the photograph of Mr. Kazimirowski's image, a print of which I am enclosing. One needs very much to retain Sister Faustina's mind [view] (the walking position, the right hand not going above the shoulder, the eyes looking downward, the rays in the direction of the viewer, and not toward the ground as in the Łagiewniki image). Sr. Faustina actually speaks of a pale [colorless] ray although sometimes she expresses herself that it's white. ...

IV.

**The matter of the correctness of the Image of
The Divine Mercy**

(Written in Bialystok, November 25, 1958)

1. Upon my request Mr. Eugene Kazimirowski began the painting of the image on January 2, 1934. Sister Faustina of blessed memory with the permission of the Superior, Mother Irene, came once or twice a week to the painter's studio (in the company of another sister) and imparted instructions, how this image is to look. For several months the painter was unable to satisfy the author, who became sad on that account, and it was at this time that she wrote in her diary: "Once

when I was at that painter's, who's painting this image, and saw, that it is not as beautiful as Jesus is, I became very sad, but I hid that deep in my heart. When we left the painter, Mother Superior remained in the city to settle various matters, but I returned home by myself, immediately I made my way to the chapel and I had a good cry. I said to the Lord: 'Who will paint You as beautiful as You are?' Of a sudden I heard the words: 'Not in the beauty of the color, nor of the brush is the greatness of this image, but in my grace'."

Mr. Kazimirowski finally asked me that I help him discharge this task and for a few days pose dressed in an alb with a cincture around the waist. This made it easier for the painter after six months to paint the image, with which Sister Faustina was on the whole satisfied, and she no longer complained about its incorrectness.

The image represents Christ in a walking posture against a dark background in a white garment, girdled by a band [belt, cincture]. With the right hand, raised to the height of the shoulder, He is blessing, and with the left one (with two fingers) he is opening the garment somewhat in the area of the Heart (not visible), from which are coming out rays (on the viewer's right a pale [colorless] one, and on the left a red one) in various directions, but principally toward the viewer. Sister Faustina called attention to this, that the right hand not be raised above the shoulder, not to bend forward, and only place the left foot forward to indicate movement, that the garment be long and somewhat fallen into folds at the bottom, that the Lord Jesus' gaze be directed a bit toward the bottom, as it happens when, standing, one looks at a point on the ground a few steps away, that the expression of the face of Jesus be gracious and merciful, that the fingers of the right hand be upright [erect] and freely lie close together, and on the left [hand] — [that] the thumb and index fingers hold the open garment; that the rays not be like ribbons [bands] hanging down toward the ground, but that with intermittent [broken] strips [streaks] they be directed toward the viewer and lightly to the sides, coloring to a certain degree the hands and surrounding objects: that these rays be transparent in such a way that through them the band [belt, cincture] and garment be visible; that the saturation of the rays with redness and whiteness [!] be greatest at the source (in the area of the Heart) and then slowly diminish and vanish [dissolve, fade away?].

2. Whether outsiders added or removed something from Sr. Faustina's statements regarding the image, I do not know, because I cannot verify it. I am rather inclined to hold that they did not do that consciously, but interpretations of that image were completely as they thought fit, not in accord with that, which is found in Sr. Faustina's Diary, and they contributed to the distortion [deformation] of the image, and in some measure of the idea itself. During Sr. Faustina's lifetime neither anyone of the Sisters of Our Lady of Mercy, nor Fr. Andrasz took any interest in the image whatever. And only after her death (in the year 1941), when they found out about the devotion to The Divine Mercy in Wilno, they instructed Mr. Hyla to paint an image, using as a model a very poor reproduction of it, executed by Mme. Balsukiewicz for a brochure with prayers (novena, chaplet and litany to The Divine Mercy), published in Krakow in 1937 (Cebulski, Szewska St. 22). Wanting to correct that reproduction, those who commissioned the image supplied the artist with incorrect indications [instructions] because they themselves did not know the details.

[I believe it needs to be pointed out that the Sisters did not commission Mr. Hyla to paint an image for them; rather, when the artist made known his desire to donate a painting for the Sister' chapel as an ex-voto for the preservation of his family and himself all during World War II, the Sisters suggested that it be a representation of the image revealed to Sr. Faustina.] — comment by Fr. Seraphim Michalenko, MIC.

Mr. Hyla painted an image of the Lord in a walking posture, but in a somewhat affectedly inclined one, against a background of flowers, with the right hand lifted high and with a gaze piercing [drilling] the viewer, with rays which, as though ribbons, hang from the heart toward the ground.

When I came [to Cracow] from Wilno (August 1947), I brought to the attention of the Sisters of Our Lady of Mercy that the image does not correspond at all to Sr. Faustina's vision, and I asked Mr Hyla to correct it and not to paint such images anymore. Unfortunately, Mr Hyla did not come into line with my observations [remarks] and said point-blank that he is going to paint the kind of images that those commissioning him are going to want, and he executed a couple hundred of them against a variety of backgrounds. Only after a few years did he begin to paint against a dark background, and, after the approval of Mr. Slendzinski's image by the principal Episcopal Commission, [he began painting the image] against the background of closed doors, without changing the posture itself, which, as was said, was incorrect.

The mistaken [incorrect] interpretation of this image is due to this, that Fr. Andrasz, not knowing the details well, in the booklet: "Divine Mercy, We Trust in You," wrote that "The Savior on this image... is walking upon this our poor earth." While in her Diary, Sr. Faustina, when she saw this image in a vision for the first time, says [See Diary, entry number 47] ... the Lord Jesus is in her cell in the evening, so that the background of the image should be dark, as it was in the Cenacle when He appeared to the Apostles with the words: "Peace to you," and instituted the sacrament of penance.

In 1953, their Excellencies the Bishops at their conference in Czestochowa decided that these images, as deriving from a private revelation, unverified by the Church, should not be accepted [for placement] in churches: those already found there should slowly be removed, in order not to anticipate the decision of the Apostolic See. At that time I made every effort to demonstrate, that this image can be treated as deriving from public revelation, for it represents Christ in the moment of instituting the sacrament of Divine Mercy (penance — Jn 20:19 ff.). It was recommended to me to have a new image painted, which Prof. Ludomir Sledzinski accomplished according to the prototype of Mr. Kazimirowski, and the Principal Episcopal Commission on 5.X.54 (on the 16th anniversary of Sr. Faustina's death) approved it as representing Christ in the moment of instituting the sacrament of penance, under the condition that it not be connected with Sr. Faustina's revelations for as long as these are not verified by the Apostolic See.

Even though this image is still not ideal, it is the closest to the Wilno prototype. Recently, upon the commission of Fr. Przybysz, a Marian (Hereford, Lower Bullingham, England) a professor from the Catholic University of Lublin, Antoni Michalak, produced a new image, more correct, with a small reservation (not the left, but the right foot is painted forward, the eyes are overly open, the background is too rich to the disadvantage of the figure itself whose countenance is somewhat sad).

3. A few years ago I wrote to Fr. Suwala and to Fr. Misiak [Pallotine priest in France, the first-named, recently deceased] that I would be swerving from the truth were I to be in agreement with what they print on the holy pictures bearing the Hyla image that they distribute: "The image painted according to Sr. Faustina's directives," because Mr. Hyla executed that image a few years after her death on the basis of instructions of persons who, during her lifetime, were not interested in this image and were completely ignorant of the details. The basic mistakes of this image are the following: the whole image reveals a showy feminism — the curved posture; the right hand raised too high; the figure's gaze skittishly drilling [the viewer], directed too high; the rays as though ropes directed towards the ground; the Savior

sometimes standing on the globe [of the earth], sometimes raised up in the clouds, which continues to be in jarring discrepancy with the prototype and the decision of their Excellencies, the Bishops. Fr. Suwala gave no response at all to my observations, and Fr. Misiak wrote back that Mr. Slendzinski's image is not liked and that is why he can't exchange it in place of My. Hyla's image.

My Hyla's stubbornness and that of the people who distribute his images is negatively disposing the Bishops to the cause of the devotion to The Divine Mercy and to me, because, as I recently found out, they impute to me that I not only tolerate this, but even support it. Up to now, in order to avoid conflict, I kept silent, but from now on for the good of the cause I have to tell the truth.

[Salutations follow.]

II.

Essential Features of
the Devotion
to The Divine Mercy

by
Rev. Ignacy Rozycki, S.T.D.

Translated by

Katherine Stackpole

II.

Essential Features of the Devotion to The Divine Mercy

Introduction

The essay published here represents a summary of the most thorough theological analysis ever written on The Divine Mercy message and devotion as revealed to the world through St. Faustina Kowalska.

The author, Fr. Ignacy Rozycki, was a theologian of considerable stature. Born near Cracow in Poland in 1911, he studied at the Pontifical University of St. Thomas Aquinas in Rome where he completed his doctorate in Dogmatic Theology. He subsequently became a leading expert on the theology of St. Thomas, and served as a member of the International Theological Commission for the Holy See.

In 1965 the then Archbishop of Cracow, Karol Wojtyla, asked Fr. Rozycki to prepare a critical analysis of the Diary and letters of Sister Faustina as part of the Informative Process concerning her life and virtues. But Fr. Rozycki initially had no inclination to waste his time examining what rumor told him were merely the hallucinations of an uneducated nun. Just before sending his refusal to the archbishop, however, he decided to glance at a copy of the Diary "just to pass the time." After reading a few passages, his prejudices against it were immediately shaken. He decided to read the entire text. The result of this second reading was evident in his actions: Fr. Rozycki applied several intense years to the task of making a thorough and systematic study of Sr. Faustina's writings. The results of his research were written in French: a massive tome of 500 pages which was presented to the Congregation for the Causes of Saints as part of the official investigation into Sr. Faustina's life and virtues. This work by Father Rozycki is presently being translated into English by the John Paul II Institute of Divine Mercy in Stockbridge, Massachusetts.

On February 19-20, 1981, at a symposium in Cracow celebrating the 50th anniversary of the revelations given to Sr.

Faustina, Fr. Rozycki delivered a lecture entitled *The Essential Features of the Devotion to The Divine Mercy* — which is here published in English for the second time (this present edition being a revision of the translation published by the Institute in 2000). In short, this essay is a compendium of the principal elements of Fr. Rozycki's main work for the Apostolic See on St. Faustina's writings. As such it is also the best survey available to date of the theology of The Divine Mercy message and devotion.

Robert A. Stackpole

Director

John Paul II Institute of Divine Mercy

Essential Features of the Devotion to The Divine Mercy

The Divine Mercy messages and devotion were recorded at Christ's command and passed on to the world in the *Diary* of Sister Helen Faustina Kowalska, a member of the Congregation of the Sisters of Our Lady of Mercy, in Poland.

There is not the slightest doubt that Divine Mercy should be the object of our adoration. When we speak of religious worship or adoration, we must always differentiate the fundamental or *proper* object from the object which is material, inessential and *relative*.[1] The principle object of any type of honor, whether religious or secular, can only be a person. The object of religious worship is always the personal God.

The personal God, God the Father, God the Son, and God the Holy Spirit, is the proper, that is the essential object of the supreme act of religious worship.[2] God alone is the object. We are permitted to adore only God Himself with acts of religious adoration. However, when our acts of worship are addressed to some created being, this veneration is not supreme worship, but only the result and expression of the supreme act of worship which we desire to direct to God Himself by venerating His created images. If we, for example, surround portraits, photographs, and other likenesses of our dear ones with signs of veneration, these representations are not in themselves the actual object of our veneration, but the persons they represent who are dear to us are the object. It is much the same with the supreme act of worship. Through sanctifying grace, every saint is a supernatural image of God, One-in-the Holy Trinity.[3] Since we are honoring God, this honor must also embrace all His images and in them find its expression, its outward manifestation. In this manner, the supreme act of adoration rendered to God, out of psychological necessity, also entails the dependent veneration of God's images. Perceived in such a manner, the acts of religious veneration do not contradict the supreme act of adoration due only to God, but directly contribute to its increase.

The place of devotion to The Divine Mercy within the scope of honor and adoration or religious worship due to God alone is defined by revealed teaching about the nature of God, One-in-the Holy Trinity. For in the light of revealed teaching, God is utterly simple, uncomplicated, absolutely having no parts. In other words, all that is within God, in His substance, is God. Thus, God is not only wise, He is Wisdom; He is not only omnipotent, He is Omnipotence. With regard to the world, He not only manifests His Providence, but He is Providence. Not only does He love us, but He is Love and not only is He merciful, but He is Mercy. Therefore, Wisdom, Providence, Omnipotence, Love and Mercy, which are the same as God, are entitled to religious adoration on our part. For this reason, there are many churches in the Christian world dedicated to St. Sophia (Holy Wisdom). Even in Poland there are churches dedicate to the Divine Providence, and in Cracow itself, there is a little Church of Divine Mercy on Smolensk Street, which in its present form dates from the year 1620. The liturgical calendar of the Catholic Church and of the separated churches honors the great works of supernatural Divine Providence: the Incarnation of the Son of God, His Nativity, His Epiphany to the nations, His Baptism, His sorrowful Passion and Death, His Resurrection, and finally the Sending of the Holy Spirit. For these were divine-human activities; and because they were divine, on our part, the supreme act of adoration is due to them.

Basically, therefore, on the part of Catholic teaching, there can be no obstacle to the worship of Divine Mercy. There remains to be solved only the question whether the form of devotion to the Divine Mercy which we find in the *Diary* of Sister Helen Faustina Kowalska is consonant with the above mentioned principles of Catholic doctrine, as well as with the fundamental centuries-old, tradition-sanctified forms of religious worship practiced by the Catholic Church. Indeed, *lex credenti lex orandi*, the rule of faith is at the same time the rule of piety, of prayer.

We must inquire, then, as to what constitutes the proper object of the Devotion to the Divine Mercy and what is its relative, material, and secondary object, according to the information conveyed by Sister Helen Faustina Kowalska. For the Divine Mercy, to whom we are to render worship in this devotion, is infinite and inexhaustible. It is, in fact, in its proper meaning as Divine Mercy, God Himself.

A question of fundamental importance arises: What concretely is denoted by the term "mercy" in those paragraphs of the *Diary* of Sister Helen Faustina that treat of the Devotion? As many as eighty-two revelations speak of the Devotion. Over half of them do not explain precisely what the object signified by this term is. However, almost half do give an explanation. In six cases "mercy" is synonymous with love; in four cases, it means the same as compassion; in four cases it denotes goodness; and finally, in four cases it signifies Jesus Himself. In these revelations mercy simultaneously means love, goodness and compassion. But within the context of the Devotion mercy takes on the Biblical meaning of the word "hesed" from the Old Testament, and of the word "eleos" from the New Testament.

Traditional Catholic moral theology treats of the virtue of mercy as a virtue flowing from love of neighbor. Namely, it is that virtue which inclines us to offer assistance to a person suffering from want or misery. This being so, "mercy" in moral theology has a narrower and secondary meaning and is not love itself but love's result and extension; it is a *pars potentialis* to the virtue of love. From this we may conclude that the mercy which we wish to honor through this Devotion and which this Devotion demands from us is simply the love of God and the love of neighbor in us.

A second conclusion of great importance flows from the fact that the mercy of which we speak in this Devotion contains a Biblical meaning. In truth, repeatedly and quite clearly, the revelations and Sister Helen Faustina call mercy a Divine attribute. We cannot explain or understand this manner of speaking in the strict philosophical-theological sense, but rather in the Biblical sense of the Old and New Testament. In the philosophical-theological sense, the characteristic or attribute of the Divine nature is that perfection, that quality, which in its essence is found in the nature of God; it is possessed by It. In this sense, all of God's attributes are God, one and the same. For this reason, all are absolutely equal to each other. Divine Mercy is as infinitely perfect as His Wisdom or Power, for it is likewise God, and the same God, just as Divine Wisdom and Divine Power are God.

If, on the other hand, mercy is understood in the Biblical sense as functional, then, even though it is called an attribute, it first of all denotes the manifestations and results of the infinite and eternal love of God in world history, and especially in the history of mankind's salvation. In fact, both *hesed* (i.e. mercy in the Old Testament) as well as *eleos* (i.e. mercy in the New Testament) signify active manifestations of God's love toward mankind. In the Old Testament the manifestations found their expression in the calling and directing of the chosen people, and in the New Testament they were found in the sending of the Son of God into the world, and in the entire work of redemption. This Biblically formulated relationship between love and mercy is expressed by Sister Helen Faustina in the words: "Love is the flower, mercy the fruit" (Diary §948), "pure love is my guide in life, but externally its fruit is mercy" (Diary §1363).

So, if we understand mercy functionally in the Biblical sense, then without any fear of error contrary to the faith, it can be said that mercy is the greatest attribute of God. For we recognize the greatest love and abyss of mercy in the Incarnation of the Word, and in His Redemption. The precise and formal sense of the statement: "Mercy is the greatest attribute of God" is that, within this biblical understanding, the results of the activity of merciful love are the greatest in the world and, in this respect, mercy surpasses all other Divine attributes. So, the meaning of this assertion is doctrinally unassailable. Its verbal formulation is probably borrowed from the Latin Vulgate, Ps. 144:9: "Miserationes eius super omnia opera eius," "His compassions (in Latin "mercies") are above all his works."

In the revelations granted to Sr. Helen Faustina, this mercy, which is love, goodness and compassion, possesses those qualities which only God can have, for it is incomprehensible, inscrutable, inexpressible, inexhaustible and infinite. In most cases in her writings, when Sr. Helen Faustina speaks of mercy, it is the mercy of Jesus. In four instances it is the mercy of Jesus' heart and in four other instances it is simply Jesus Himself. In only four cases does it appear as the mercy of God the Father; and in two cases as the Mercy of God, One-in-the Trinity. The mercy of God the Father appears first and foremost in the Chaplet of Divine Mercy, which is one of the main forms of this Devotion. Its sense also includes the mercy of Jesus' human heart as is found by the words of the 25th revelation: "Divine mercy through the divine-human heart of Jesus" (Diary §528).

In virtue of a basic commandment of natural moral law, we have the obligation to worship God in every possible, appropriate manner, that is, with the supreme act of worship, the worship of adoration. Divine Mercy demands from us the ultimate religious worship and adoration since every Divine activity is simply God, because of God's absolute simplicity. The question arises: In what sense does Divine Mercy, (understood as above), appear as the object of that devotion which the Lord Jesus wished to inculcate into His Church by means of Sister Helen Faustina? The most general answer to this is found in the words of Jesus related to His formal demand for the veneration of the image described in the initial revelation of February 22, 1931: "I demand the worship of Mercy... through the veneration of this image."[4] The words of Jesus, cited above, distinguish two objects of the Devotion, namely, its essential or proper object, and it inessential, incidental, and material object. The words "through the veneration of this image" unmistakenly indicate that the image whose painting and veneration Jesus demanded was to be only a means for honoring Mercy, consequently, only its material, inessential object. The proper object, in other words, the object to which all acts and forms of devotion are in reality directed, is Mercy alone.

As we have already emphasized, this mercy is the Divine, infinite and unfathomable Mercy of God, one-in-Holy Trinity, the mercy of God the Father, but most especially and most often the mercy of Jesus Christ or His Divine-human Heart. Although, the mercy of the Sacred Heart of Jesus simply and directly signifies the human, created mercy by which His Heart was guided and lived for us, nevertheless on the basis of the unity of personality, it also signifies His Divine Mercy. Concerning His Sacred Heart, Jesus speaks to Sister Helen Faustina: "My Heart is Mercy Itself" (Diary §1777). But He also states the same thing about Himself. Therefore, Jesus as the incarnation of Divine Mercy is also the proper object of the devotion. It follows that this Devotion may equally well be called Devotion to the Divine Mercy and Devotion to the Merciful Jesus, with both names expressing exactly the essence of the Devotion in reference to its object.

Jesus, the Divine Mercy Incarnate, occupies, however, a privileged place in this Devotion. He is not only the proper object of it, but He is the main object, in the sense that all acts of this Devotion actually have Jesus as the proper aim, even those acts which are directed to the other Persons of God. For instance, the Chaplet of the Divine Mercy is clearly directed to the Mercy of God the Father. However, the 31st and 49th revelations (Diary §687 and §848) represent Jesus as the one who bestows all graces associated with this chaplet. Furthermore, He is presented as the object of the trust in Mercy which we express by reciting the chaplet. This exceptional place of Jesus within the framework of the Devotion has its doctrinal basis in the words of the Gospel: "I am the Way, the Truth, and the Life. No one goes to the Father except through Me." Since Jesus is the main object of this Devotion, it may rightly be called in a shortened form the Devotion to the Merciful Lord Jesus.

However, the Mercy of God, One-in-Holy Trinity, God the Father and Jesus, is not only the proper object of this Devotion but it is also its motive. The extraordinary, truly Divine characteristics of this Mercy are the incentive which inclines us to the basic, most essential act of the Devotion: namely, to unshaken and unlimited trust in The Divine Mercy. For Divine Love and Mercy embrace the whole world in such a way that "everything which exists emerged from the bowels of My Mercy" (Diary §699). Not only did it emerge when it was created through an act of Divine Love, but also "everything that exists is permanent, is contained in the bowels of My Mercy, more deeply than an infant in the womb of its mother," as we read in revelation 46 (Diary §1076). In interpersonal relations, we know of no more beautiful nor touching love than that of a mother for her child. The words of the Lord Jesus quoted above figuratively emphasize that the love of God toward mankind is greater and more tender than the greatest love we can experience from people; and this being so, it deserves that we take towards it the attitude of unwavering trust. Furthermore, the consequence of the greatness of Divine Mercy is His care for the affairs of all those who trust in Him. This actually is the principle of God's Mercy. We read, for example, in revelation 35: "Whoever trusts in My Mercy will not perish, for all his concerns are mine" (Diary §723). In revelation 56 Jesus says: "The soul that placed its trust in my mercy is the most fortunate, for I personally care for it" (Diary §1273). This same idea is most strongly expressed in revelation 76: "Sooner would heaven and earth vanish, than a trusting soul not be enveloped by Divine Mercy" (Diary §1777).

Three very characteristic, attractive and interrelated Divine attributes flow from the most fundamental essence of Divine Mercy: (1) "The greater the misery, the greater its right to My Mercy" (Diary §1182), (2) "The greater the sinner, the greater his right to My Mercy" (Diary §598), (3) "I am more generous to sinners than to the righteous" (Diary §1275).

On the one hand, it is evident that the greater the misery, the more assistance it requires. Mercy for its part hastens with assistance especially to all those who need it more, particularly those whose misery is greatest. For, when giving assistance, inviolable moral law requires that priority be given to those who need it more. The Lord Jesus applied this principle to God the Father when He said, "I tell you that there will be more joy in heaven from the conversion of one sinner, than from ninety-nine of the righteous who need no repentance." In accord with this essential attribute of mercy, the Lord Jesus assures us in revelation 77 that: "the greatest misery of the soul does not incite My anger, but My heart is moved with great mercy toward it" (Diary §1739). In revelation 69, we learn: "I am happy when they demand much, because it is My desire to grant much, very much" (Diary §1578).

It is evident to every believing Catholic that the infinite Mercy of God is inexhaustible. The greatest sins, not only of an individual person, but those of the entire world, will neither exhaust it, nor ever equal it. Likewise the Divine-human mercy of the heart of Jesus is inexhaustible. Jesus speaks of it in revelation 56: "It [Divine Mercy] increases through giving itself" (Diary §1273). At first glance this is an extraordinary argument, but in reality it is profoundly theological It refers to the universally accepted contention of moral theology that all virtues grow through performance of those acts to which they incline. Consequently, we find no basis for the exhaustion of the Divine-human Mercy of the Heart of Jesus. In the whole history of Catholic theology, no one has given a deeper reason for the inexhaustibility of the Divine-human Mercy of the Heart of Jesus.

Comparison with Devotion to the Sacred Heart

It is possible to conduct a comparison between this Devotion and the Devotion to the Sacred Heart of Jesus based on what has already been said about the object of Devotion to Divine Mercy. It might appear that there is no essential difference between these two devotions, and that the Devotion to the Sacred Heart of Jesus can be found within the framework of Devotion to Divine Mercy. Do we not say in the litany to the Sacred Heart of Jesus that it is full of love and goodness, that it is long-suffering and of great mercy, that it is generous to all who call upon it?

Such a view of the relationship between these two devotions would, however, be shallow and not in accord with the essential features of either devotion. The essential and proper object of the Devotion to the Sacred Heart of Jesus is the Divine person of the Incarnate Son of God. Meanwhile, the proper object of Devotion to the Divine Mercy is Divine Mercy in the Holy Trinity, God the Father and the Son of God, Jesus. Divine Mercy is the personal God and can, therefore, be the object of the supreme act of religious worship. In consequence, the proper object of Devotion to Divine Mercy is different in its scope and wider than the proper object of Devotion to the Sacred Heart of Jesus. The human, bodily Heart of Jesus is the material object of Devotion to the [Sacred] Heart of Jesus. In revelations concerning Devotion to Divine Mercy, there is repeatedly talk about the Sacred Heart of Jesus as the seat of inexhaustible Mercy, but never is the Heart itself presented as the material object of the Devotion.[5] Rather, the material object in the Devotion to Divine Mercy is a physical image corresponding to the vision of February 22, 1931. Devotion to the Sacred Heart of Jesus requires from us, above all, acts of reparation for sinful offenses, while acts of unshaken trust in God are the very essence of Devotion to Divine Mercy. Devotion to the Sacred Heart of Jesus has its privileged days: the first Fridays of each month, and the Feast of the Sacred Heart of Jesus on the Friday after the octave of Corpus Christi. By contrast, Devotion to The Divine Mercy, with the exception of the Feast of Mercy which is to fall on the first Sunday after Easter, has no special day. On the contrary, it has a special hour, namely, 3:00 p.m., each day of the year. In spite of the fact that small alterations would suffice to adapt the Litany to the Sacred Heart of Jesus for use as a devotion to Divine Mercy, nonetheless these two devotions are different, both in their essential disposition as well as in their manifestations.

Fundamental Essence of Devotion to The Divine Mercy

Before discussing concrete forms of Devotion to Divine Mercy, it is necessary to answer the question: What constitutes the fundamental essence of Devotion to The Divine Mercy?. Trust constitutes this [essence] to such a degree that without trust there is no devotion such as Jesus wished, and without trust, it is impossible to attain any of the promises attached to the Devotion. Trust is a basic and essential act of this Devotion to such a degree that it alone, without any other concrete forms of the Devotion, is already a guarantee of achieving all the general promises Jesus attached to this Devotion. We submit that trust in this sense is essential and necessary from the fact that Jesus not only insists on it thirty-four times, but also because He speaks of it nine times as a condition necessary for attaining the benefits ensuing from the Devotion: "The graces of My Mercy may be drawn by one vessel alone, which is trust" (Diary §1578). This principle refers not only to sanctifying and saving grace, but also to temporal benefits, which is attested by revelation 13: "Mankind will not have peace until it turns with trust to My Mercy" (Diary §300).

The result is that no external action of this Devotion generates any of the results promised by Jesus unless the action expresses trust and is carried out with trust. For example, if one says the Chaplet of Divine Mercy without trust, he or she will not receive in return any of the blessings Jesus promised to one's reciting the Chaplet with trust. Likewise, if the veneration given to the Image of Divine Mercy does not spring from an actual worship of Mercy, Jesus will not grant any of the graces attendant to the veneration of the Image, for to honor Divine Mercy implies turning to Him with an act of trust. Because the veneration of Mercy is the same as trust, Jesus could direct this call and warning to all: "If souls do not honor My Mercy, they will perish for all ages" (Diary §965). The necessity of trust is indispensable not only for personal salvation, but also for the propitious development and peace of all mankind: "Mankind will have no peace, until it turns with trust to My Mercy" (Diary §300).

For the same reason, trust alone in Mercy, without any of the concrete acts of devotion as revealed through Sister Helen Faustina, assures achievement of all normal effects of the Devotion as we read in revelation 35: "Whoever trusts My Mercy will not perish, for all his affairs are Mine" (Diary §723). "All" refers not only to salvation and sanctification, but also to temporal prosperity and fortune. Jesus says the same thing in different words in revelation 56: "A soul which trusts in My Mercy is the most fortunate, for I personally care for it" (Diary §1273). In revelation 66 we are assured that "no soul which called upon My Mercy was ever disappointed, nor ever put to shame" (Diary §1541). However, for the attainment of the extraordinary graces attached by Jesus to some of the devotional acts, it is an indispensable necessity to perform the acts. For example: Whoever desires to experience complete remission of all sins and punishment, must receive Holy Communion on the Feast of Mercy, that is, the first Sunday of Easter.

What is This Trust?

What is this trust in which the essence of Devotion to Divine Mercy consists? Trust cannot be understood as an emotion or attitude in isolation from the whole of Christian life. Rather, it is the attitude which the Lord Jesus called faith and which He expected from His followers when He said: "If you have faith like a mustard seed, you will tell this mountain, 'Go from here over there' and it will move. And nothing will be impossible for you" (Mt 17:20). This same attitude of life is described by St. Paul and by the whole of Christian theology as hope, the divine virtue of hope which springs from living faith in the infinity of God's love and goodness toward us. It is indissolubly tied to humility, that is the sincere and deep conviction that all good within us and which we do is the work and gift of God; that we possess nothing except that which we have from God. This trust-hope constitutes the opening of a soul's receiving Divine grace, and the requesting of it is an attitude of continuous and most effective prayer. In revelations concerning the Devotion, the Lord Jesus links this attitude of hope with repentance for sins to such a degree that He clearly calls upon devotees of Divine Mercy to strive for the deepest possible trust and repentance as often as they receive the sacrament of Confession. Thus confession, a common Christian activity, becomes an act of devotion to Mercy.

Great promises belong to the essence of the Devotion, but there are also certain requirements. In the first place, an indispensably necessary element of the Devotion is an active love of neighbor or the practice of mercy toward our neighbor. The Lord Jesus applies the principle to the Devotion. It is a principle which He expounded in all its extent and without the slightest mitigation during His lifetime, and which is found in revelation 36, dated October 24, 1936: "If a soul does not perform mercy in some manner, then it shall not know My Mercy on the Judgment Day" (Diary §1317).[6] Jesus repeated His call four times: in revelations 36, 51, 52, and 58 (Diary §742, 1317,

1148, 1158), incorporating what He had said in the Sermon on the Mount: "Blessed are the merciful, for they shall obtain mercy" (Mt 5:17). Explaining this demand, the Lord Jesus stressed that mercy of "spirit" has greater "merit" and added that if a person cannot show mercy by action, then let the person at least practice it in word. If he or she cannot practice it in word, let the person practice it by prayer, for everyone can always pray. The Lord Jesus expressed clearly that He wishes each devotee of Divine Mercy to perform each day at least one act of mercy toward one's neighbor, through a good deed, a good word, or through prayer. In this way, the Devotion to Divine Mercy which Jesus wishes to spread through the mediation of Sister Faustina, cannot be artificial religiosity, but rather a deeply experienced form of the Christian religious life.

The basic requirement of performing acts of mercy toward one's neighbor is actually fulfilled by all the concrete forms of the Devotion to Divine Mercy. The Chaplet of Mercy was arranged in such a fashion by the Lord Jesus that it is an act of mercy toward neighbors, for Jesus instructs us to pray for mercy not only for ourselves or those close to us, but for the entire world. That is why, when He promises a happy death in God's grace to those who trustingly and with humility of heart would say this Chaplet even once, He was not making an exception with regard to the basic requirement of mercy toward neighbors.

Before we familiarize ourselves with the concrete forms of Devotion to Mercy, we should note that among the concrete forms we do not find commonly known novenas or litanies. Those who come in contact with the Devotion to the Divine Mercy for the first time most often inquire about novenas and litanies. In the Diary of Sister Helen Faustina we admittedly do find a very beautiful and profound novena to Divine Mercy which, according to Sister Helen Faustina's accounts, was given to her by the Lord Jesus, but this novena was intended for Sister Helen Faustina herself, and not for everyone. The

Lord Jesus attached no special promise to its recitation. This should be remembered as often as it is recited. It is a beautiful and profound prayer for the salvation of different categories of people and, in this regard, it is an act of spiritual mercy toward our neighbors. If, beyond this, it is recited with such trust as demanded by the Lord Jesus in the devotion, it would be an authentic act of the Devotion to which may be applied the promise attached by Christ to trust in Divine Mercy.

Sister Helen Faustina composed and bequeathed to us in her *Diary* a litany[7] to The Divine Mercy. Another litany to Divine Mercy is found in a Cracowian, post-synodal prayer book, *Sluzmy Bogu.* While two litanies to The Divine Mercy already exist, then there is nothing to prevent the composition of yet another, perhaps even a more beautiful one than those already in existence. We need to remember, however, that the Lord Jesus did not attach any special promise to the recitation of the litany. If however, someone recites this litany or another with the required trust and works of mercy, he or she can only count on what the Lord Jesus generally attached to acts of trust in Mercy.

In the course of relaying to Sister Helen Faustina His will regarding this Devotion, Christ did in fact demand the recitation of novenas from Sister Helen Faustina and her wards. These novenas were always novenas of Chaplets of The Divine Mercy. All the more, it should be remembered that Christ attached extraordinarily great promises to the recitation of the Chaplet. He gave it such great effectiveness that "through this Chaplet everything can be gained," if such is the will of God.

FORMS OF DEVOTION AND PROMISES

If the devotee of Divine Mercy is to be guaranteed all the benefits which the Lord Jesus attached to this Devotion, every act of veneration of The Divine Mercy must be an expression of trust and must be linked to the practice of mercy toward ones neighbor. These basic conditions should never be forgotten.

VENERATION OF THE IMAGE OF
THE MERCIFUL CHRIST

Christ began the revelation of the Devotion [to Divine Mercy] to Sister Helen Faustina and to the world on February 22, 1931, with an evening apparition in her convent cell in Plock [I saw the Lord Jesus clothed in a white garment. One hand raised in the gesture of blessing, the other was touching the garment at the breast. From beneath the garment, slightly drawn aside at the breast, there were emanating two large rays, one red and one pale. After a while, Jesus said to me: "Paint an image according to the pattern you see, with the signature, Jesus, I Trust in You. I desire that this image be venerated first in your chapel, and [then] throughout the world. I promise that the soul that will venerate this image will not perish. I also promise victory over [its] enemies already here on earth, and especially at the hour of death. I Myself will defend it as My own glory" (Diary 47-48)].

The artist-painter, Adolf Hyla of Krakowskie Łagiewniki (d.1965) painted the image of the Merciful Lord Jesus, reproducing the figure of Jesus from the Plock vision. It is this image that is venerated by the Sisters of Our Lady of Mercy in their chapel in Łagiewniki, Cracow, where Sister Helen Faustina lived and died. It is also the Image which is reproduced and disseminated in many of the periodicals propagating this Devotion.

The image, however, requires some comments. First of all, the rays which Sister Helen Faustina saw at Plock were not red and white in color, but one was red, and the other was pale. Therefore, the Plock revelation, and the Devotion based on it, do not utilize the Polish national colors. It is not infected with nationalism and it is not patriotism under the guise of piety. The second ray cannot be white, but should be pale, since white conflicts with the symbolic interpretation of the rays. The Lord explained to Sister Helen Faustina that the two rays found in this image symbolize the Water and Blood which flowed from the pierced side of Christ. However, the watery liquid flowing from Christ's side, which was seen by Christ's beloved disciple and which he wrote about in the Gospel, was partially mixed with blood and, according to the opinion of Biblical scholars, was pale in color, slightly rust-colored and similar to a person's pale complexion.

Jesus Himself, in describing the two rays of Mercy, told Sister Helen Faustina "through you, the rays of Mercy will pass into the world." He related the meaning of the rays with the deep symbolism of water and blood which, according to the Gospel of St. John (19:34-37), flowed from the side of Christ. In the light of the entire Gospel of John, the water and blood flowing from the pierced side of Christ symbolize the graces of the Holy Spirit who was given to us as a result of Christ's death. The two rays on the image of the Merciful Jesus ultimately possess this same profound meaning.

The Image of Divine Mercy painted by A. Hyla is at variance with the Plock vision of the Merciful Jesus in one detail, namely, the second ray on it is distinctly white. While it is unusually difficult to represent a watery liquid, as well as a pale ray, with paint, for the good of the Devotion, it is necessary to strive toward this. Nevertheless, one should anticipate that the Lord Jesus will reconcile Himself to the fact that the artistic rendition will not fulfill His intentions nor those of the artist. The Lord Jesus is concerned with the essence and not with secondary details. He is concerned that the image expresses our trust and the Mercy of Jesus, the source of which is His death. Jesus will reconcile Himself to such an artistic shortcoming in the same manner as He reconciled Himself to the deficiencies of the first image painted at Vilnius in 1934 by E. Kazimirowski. The deficiencies not only caused sadness but even weeping in Sister Helen Faustina.

Jesus demanded that the Image, as the object of veneration in the Devotion, bear the inscription "Jesus, I Trust in You! [Jezu Ufam Tobie]" and that it be placed under and not above the painting. Christ did not, however, place as an irrevocably necessary condition that the inscription repeat the three words [Jezu Ufam Tobie] exactly and literally. After all, Christ offered the Devotion to The Divine Mercy to the whole world, to all nations who speak in diverse tongues. Consequently, Jesus was certainly concerned with the meaning and not the number of words. He was concerned that the same idea be expressed, even if the words varied. Revelation 21 suggests that an image representing the crucified Christ with two rays emerging from His pierced side with the inscription, "Jesus, I Trust in You," would be equally acceptable as an object of veneration, in accordance with the intentions of Jesus Christ, and that it would enjoy the same promises as the Image at Łagiewniki. The salvific value of Christ's death, which is the source of Mercy, would be even more perceptible and its meaning more understandable.

Christ demanded public veneration of the Image of Mercy, in churches, and not only in the private dwellings of the laity, priests or religious. Christ did not explain in full detail what this public veneration of the Image should be. Given that Jesus desired that the Image be solemnly consecrated (blessed) and venerated by the faithful in church, and not beyond the enclosure, one can presume that He expects signs of veneration for this Image similar to the veneration given to other paintings in churches, chapels, and private homes.

The Image of the Merciful Jesus is to play a double role in the Devotion. First, for the Lord Jesus, it is an instrument through which graces are distributed. We know that it is not the Image giving graces, but Jesus through the Image. The Image does not have autonomous power. For the people, however, the Image is to serve as a vessel for drawing graces from the wellspring of Mercy.

Second, by the explicit will of Jesus, the Image is to be a sign which is to bring to mind Christ's demand for performing acts of mercy. Since this second function of the Image is often forgotten, and the veneration alone without deeds of mercy is not the Devotion required by Christ, worshipers of Mercy should conform to Christ's demand so that they let no day pass without performing at least one act of mercy: by deed, word, or prayer.

A practical, clear and very important conclusion flows from the second function of the Image: Jesus awaits and demands that the prayer of trust before the image of the Merciful Jesus be combined with an examination of conscience, an examination of how we have fulfilled Christ's demands to perform at least one deed of mercy daily.

There are two components in the promises connected with this veneration: what Christ promised distinctly and what He promised indistinctly. In the inaugural revelation of February 22, 1931, Christ assured, "that the soul that will venerate this Image will not perish." Christ, therefore, attached the promise of everlasting salvation to the veneration of this Image.

Christ promised that those who venerate the Image would achieve great progress along the road to holiness gaining victory in this life over the enemies of the soul and enemies of salvation. He promised a happy and holy death with the assurance that He personally would defend them as His glory at the hour of their death.

The range of promises not directly named by Jesus was defined by the first role of the Image, i.e., that of a vessel for drawing graces from the wellspring of Mercy, but subordinated to trust. Consequently, we will obtain more quickly and in a much greater degree all the saving graces and all the temporal benefits which it is possible to obtain through unwavering trust in Divine Mercy, if we express this trust in the form of veneration of the Image. If the Lord Jesus assured us that, "I wish to grant unimaginable graces to those who trust in My Mercy," then this certainly, first of all, refers to the veneration accorded to the Image of Divine Mercy. Finally, Christ did not delineate any limits to the size of greatness of the graces and temporal benefits which we can expect through veneration, with unwavering trust, of the Image of the Divine Mercy.

THE FEAST OF MERCY

The Feast of Divine Mercy occupies the first place among all external manifestations of the Devotion. The Lord Jesus let us know His will in the inaugural revelation. In order to have this feast day established, He devoted fourteen (14) of His revelations to it. He requested of Sister Helen Faustina that the feast be preceded by a novena consisting of the Chaplet of the Divine Mercy. He attached such importance to this feast that in the 43rd revelation He stated: "My Heart rejoices on account of this Feast" (Diary §998). The Feast of Divine Mercy is to be celebrated on the first Sunday after Easter. The selection of this Sunday, as well as the distinct desire of Jesus that priests preach sermons about the Divine Mercy on this day (especially about the Mercy that God grants us through Christ), all serve to indicate that Jesus sees an integral relation between the Paschal mystery of our redemption and this Feast. Christ intended that we contemplate the mystery of Redemption on that day as the greatest manifestation of Divine Mercy toward us. This relationship between the Feast of Divine Mercy and the mystery of Redemption was also noted by Sister Helen Faustina when she wrote in 1935: "Now I see that the work of Redemption is connected with the work of Mercy, which the Lord demands" (Diary §89).

Such a feast is not found in the liturgical calendar of the universal Church nor in that of the Church in Poland.[8] The agreement of such a feast with the teaching of the Catholic faith has already been established at the beginning of this presentation. The liturgical rules of the post-conciliar Missal and Breviary only seem, on the surface, to exclude such a feast on the first Sunday after Easter. In fact, there exists a rule which precludes the liturgical celebration of any feast day or solemnity on the Sunday after Easter. If, however, we examine closely the post-conciliar Missal, we will notice that the Mass formulary for the second Sunday of Easter already says very much and with such clarity about the greatness of Divine Mercy, that with only slight changes it can serve as a Mass dedicated to Divine Mercy. Also, the post-conciliar Breviary reading for this Sunday can easily become a public and a liturgical meditation and veneration of Divine Mercy. For instance, we could take the second reading from the Office of Readings and replace it with a reading from the papal encyclical of John Paul II, *Dives in Misericordia*. The appropriate section which discusses Divine Mercy as manifested in the Cross and Resurrection could be used. Since the writings and homilies of Pope Paul VI have found a place in the post-conciliar Breviary, by this same token there is also room for the encyclicals of John Paul II.

As we have said, Jesus demands that the Feast of The Divine Mercy be preceded by a novena, and He required Sister Helen Faustina to prepare for its celebration by means of a novena consisting of the recitation of the Chaplet of The Divine Mercy. The novena of Chaplets of The Divine Mercy unites within itself, on the one hand, the promises of Jesus dependent on the recitation of this Chaplet and, on the other hand, those attached to celebrating the novena prior to The Feast of Divine Mercy. Referring to the novena, Jesus said: "Through this novena, I will bestow all possible graces upon souls" (Diary §796). The words "all possible graces" mean that the person saying the novena to the Divine Mercy will obtain all the benefits of God he asks for, regardless of whether he requests these graces for himself or for others.

Jesus demands that the Feast be celebrated solemnly, as a liturgical feast of the universal Church. As to the means of celebration, He expressed two wishes. In the first place, the Image of Divine Mercy is to be ceremoniously blessed on this feast day, and it also is to be publicly, that is liturgically, venerated on this Sunday. In the second place, "On that day, priests should speak to souls of this grace and unfathomable Mercy of Mine" (Diary §570).

Jesus demands, therefore, that the subject of this day's sermon be His Mercy, not only His Divine and infinite Mercy, but also the unimaginable Mercy of His human Heart, above all attested to by His Passion, for He wants "the Feast of Mercy to be a recourse and a refuge for all souls, but especially for all sinners." Since there is no other means of drawing graces from the wellspring of Mercy but through trust, the sermon should be such that it might incite the audience to a posture of unwavering and fervent trust. A priest can only prove equal to this demand if he shows the faithful the unfathomable love and mercy of Jesus, both in His Passion and in the entire work of Redemption. Thus, the proper aim of this feast is the recapitulation of the entire work of Redemption from the point of view of Mercy.[9]

In sermons given on this day, it is proper to mention the most exceptional grace which Jesus attached to the celebration of this Feast in revelation 13: "Whoever receives the Source of Life on this day will attain complete remission of sins and punishment" (Diary §300). He repeated this promise even more clearly in revelation 33: "Whichever soul goes to Confession and receives Holy Communion, such a soul will attain complete remission of sins and punishment" (Diary §699).

The most exceptional grace promised by Jesus for the Feast of the Divine Mercy is something considerably greater than a plenary indulgence. The latter consists only of the remission of temporal punishments for committed sins, but is never the remission of sins itself. The exceptional grace of [the Communion on] Divine Mercy Sunday is also greater than the graces of the other sacraments, with the exception of the Sacrament of Baptism, for the remission of all sins and punishment is only found in the sacramental grace of Baptism. In the promises cited, Christ tied the remission of all sins and punishment to the reception of Holy Communion on the Feast of Divine Mercy. The grace of the complete remission of sins and punishment is theologically possible since neither this grace, nor the conditions for obtaining it contradict revealed teachings. If God is able to bestow this grace through the sacrament of Baptism, why would He not be able to bestow it—if He so wishes—through the Eucharist, which is the greatest sacrament? And the requirement of trust, expressed in two of the revelations regarding the Feast of Mercy (*Diary*, §§ 299, 300, and § 699), and absolutely necessary for every act of the Divine Mercy Devotion, isn't it only a reminder of Sacred Scripture? What is more, the greatness of this grace is capable of bringing to life in us a boundless trust, which Jesus desires so much for us on this day of Mercy.

The nature of this highest grace leaves no room for any ambiguity: It is the complete remission of sins and punishment; in other words: It is the complete forgiveness of all sins, which were not yet forgiven and of all punishment due for those sins. As regards the forgiveness of sins then, this grace is equal to the grace of Baptism. In other words, Jesus raised the reception of Holy Communion on the Feast of The Divine Mercy to the rank of a "second Baptism."[10]

[NOTE: Please do not omit to examine carefully this very important footnote.]

It is obvious that in order to effect a complete forgiveness of sins and punishment, the Holy Communion received on the Feast of Divine Mercy must not only be partaken of worthily, but it must also fulfill the basic requirements of the Divine Mercy devotion. However, received unworthily, without trust in Divine Mercy and devoid of some deed of mercy toward neighbor, it would be a contradiction of Devotion to the Divine Mercy. Instead of the exceptional grace, it would bring down upon the recipient the Divine Wrath. The spiritual good of the faithful demands that they know what graces they can obtain and under what conditions through the reception of Holy Communion on the Feast of Divine Mercy.

Jesus did not limit His generosity on the Feast of Divine Mercy exclusively to this one, supreme grace. On the contrary, He declared that "on that day, the bowels of My Mercy are open: I pour out a whole ocean of graces upon souls who will approach the fount of My Mercy ...On that day are opened all the Divine floodgates through which graces flow" (Diary §699). For this reason, "let no soul fear to approach Me." From these words of Christ, it is evident that He fervently desires the Feast of Divine Mercy to be an unusually effective refuge for all mankind, especially for sinners, incomparably more effective than all other forms of Devotion to The Divine Mercy.

The incomparable effectiveness of this refuge is manifested in three ways. First it is manifested through its universality. All people, even those who never had devotion to The Divine Mercy, even sinners who repented on the day of the Feast itself, can participate to the fullest extent in all the graces which Jesus prepared for this Feast. Secondly, on this day, Jesus wishes to shower people not only with saving graces, but also with temporal blessings, both to individuals and to communities of people, for He said: "Mankind will not know peace until it turns to the fount of My Mercy." Thirdly, all graces and benefits, even in their highest degrees, are accessible on this day to everyone, as long as they are asked for with great trust. Christ did not attach such an extraordinary abundance of graces and benefits to any other form of this Devotion.

THE CHAPLET OF THE DIVINE MERCY

Since the Lord Jesus devoted fourteen revelations to the

Divine Mercy Chaplet, it indicates that its value is not far behind the Feast of the Divine Mercy.

The structure of the Chaplet is perfectly clear. It begins with the recitation of the Our Father, the Hail Mary, and the Creed. This is followed by five decades which should be said on ordinary rosary beads. Each decade begins with the words: "Eternal Father, I offer You the Body and Blood, Soul and Divinity of Your dearly beloved Son, our Lord Jesus Christ, in atonement for our sins and those of the whole world." These words should be said on the large beads. Next, on the small beads we should pray ten times the words: "For the sake of His sorrowful Passion, have mercy on us and on the whole world."

Before any further considerations, we should establish the meaning of the two prayers. What is the meaning of the introductory words, "I offer You the Body and Blood, Soul and Divinity of Our Lord Jesus Christ"? First, it is certain that this form is entirely in accord with Catholic teaching of the Faith. [This is evident] because this same wording is found in the prayer dictated to Lucy and her companions by an Angel at Fatima in 1916. The Church has recognized the supernatural origin of the Fatima revelations, a fact which could not have transpired if the wording was either contrary to the Faith or dangerous to it. Consequently historical precedent supports the complete correctness of the introductory words of the Divine Mercy Chaplet. These words also find support in the logical analysis of their substance. Based on the fundamental principle of textual interpretation, the meaning of words is usually and finally described by the context in which they appear. Let us, therefore, notice that what we offer to God the Father by these words is not Divinity, pure and simple and without any other explanations and descriptions. In other words, what is being offered is not the Divine nature shared in common by the Father, Son, and Holy Spirit. By the formulation, we offer the Divinity of Jesus Christ, and according to the teaching of the Church and theologians, the Divinity of Jesus Christ in point of fact directly and immediately indicates the Divinity proper to Jesus, as differentiated from the Divinity of the Father. Therefore, it is the same as His Divine Person. The whole formulation taken in its entirety ("Body and Blood, Soul and Divinity of Jesus Christ") signifies the wholeness of the Person of Jesus Christ, the Son of God Incarnate. In other words, we are offering both His Divine Personality and His Humanity composed of body and soul.

The whole Person of the Incarnate Son of God can be offered by us to God the Father since, according to the letter to the Ephesians. God the Son Himself, fulfilling the mission entrusted to Him by God, "delivered Himself up for us as an offering and a sacrifice" (Eph 5:2). From this Pauline text, it follows that the object of the sacrifice offered to God the Father by Christ was Christ Himself, namely, His entire humanity as well as His Divine Person. As we say the Chaplet and recite these words, we unite ourselves with the Sacrifice of the Cross offered by Jesus for our salvation. And when we emphasize in this wording that it is precisely the dearly beloved Son that we offer to the Father, then we appeal to the love bestowed by the eternal Father on His Son suffering for us. In consequence, we also appeal to the love of the eternal Father for all mankind, namely, that love which found its highest expression in the sorrowful Passion of Jesus. In other words, we turn to the strongest motive in order to be heard by God.

"For the sake of His sorrowful Passion" is not an appeal to the satisfaction which Jesus offered for our sins. Fidelity to the spirit and letter of the Devotion demands rather an appeal to the love and Mercy of the Father and Son for us, and to that love which is attested by the sufferings of the Son. In other words, we again emphasize the strongest motive upon which the efficacy of the Chaplet is based; we briefly call: "May so much hardship, so much suffering not be in vain." We repeat the same idea which Thomas of Celano expressed in the hymn, Dies Irae: "Exhausted You sought me, crucified You saved me, may

Your Wounds not be in vain."

Fidelity to the text of the Chaplet and to the spirit of the Devotion demands the continual petition for Mercy "on us and on the whole world," i.e., to use the plural "us" always. The "us" signifies the person reciting the prayer, as well as all those for whom the person especially wishes and is obliged to pray. The "whole world," on the other hand, includes all living people and all the souls in purgatory. Even if we recite the Chaplet individually, we should still employ the plural form, "on us and on the whole world." Acting thus, we execute an act of mercy, which, as explained earlier, is a condition necessary for the reception of Mercy from God. If someone should pray the Chaplet and request mercy only for himself, it would be contrary to the will of Christ and would not be an act of the Devotion. The person praying would not gain those benefits which Christ attached to the recitation of the Chaplet.

Perseverance should characterize the recitation of the Chaplet as an external expression of our internal trust in Divine Mercy. In truth, Jesus did promise twice (in revelations 48 and 66, Diary §1128 and §1541) that it is possible to obtain everything through this Chaplet. Nonetheless, with the exception of the grace of a good death, He never promised instant results after a single recitation. In the revelations received by Sister Helen Faustina, we find examples of both: a single Chaplet being sufficient to guarantee a dying person a good and peaceful death, as well as examples which show that to achieve this same goal one must repeat the Chaplet more than once, persistently and at length, without discouragement that we have not been heard immediately. The letter and spirit of the Devotion demand this of us, but so do the teaching of Jesus in the Gospel: "It is necessary to pray always, and never to cease" (Lk 18:1).

Jesus attached a great general promise as well as unusual specific promises to the recitation of the Chaplet.

The general promise was given in the 48th revelation and repeated in the 66th: "Through the recitation of this Chaplet, it pleases Me to grant everything that will be asked of Me." Jesus' explanation of revelation 66 is as follows: "Through it, you will be granted everything, as long as what you ask for is in accordance with My will" (Diary §1541). For all that is contrary to God's will is either evil or harmful. That is why it cannot be granted by the most-Good, and most-Blessed God. The "everything" of Christ's promise signifies saving grace as well as temporal benefits for the individual persons and for communities.

Sister Helen Faustina, at the command of Christ, made novenas of the Chaplet in order to "appease her Father and obtain Mercy for Poland." In the first place, however, spiritual benefits, graces, are the main object of the general promise attached to the Chaplet ("The bowels of My Mercy are moved on behalf of all reciting the chaplet." Diary §848). Obviously, under two conditions: if the persons saying the Chaplet manifest great trust and perseverance; and if they perform works of mercy.

The exceptional greatness of the graces and benefits promised by Christ to those saying the Divine Mercy Chaplet is evident in the four special promises.

The first of these special promises was granted in September of 1936: "Whoever recites it will attain great mercy at the hour of death....Even the most hardened sinner, if he only once says this chaplet, will receive grace from My infinite mercy" (Diary 687). Christ is here referring to the grace of conversion and a God- fearing death in the state of Divine grace. The exceptional greatness of Christ's Mercy is based on the fact that the only condition for receiving it is that a person say this Chaplet once, entirely the way Jesus established it, along with dispositions consistent with the meaning of the prayers which make it up, above all with trust, humility, and repentance for sins. This first special promise is directed to all mankind. The three remaining promises are reserved for the dying. Revelation 39, dated

December 12, 1936, grants this same grace of conversion and remission of sins to the dying if the Chaplet to The Divine Mercy is recited at their bedside: "if others recite it at the side of the dying, then the latter will receive this same grace of remission. When this Chaplet is said at the side of the dying, the wrath of God is appeased, and unfathomable Mercy encompasses the soul" (Diary §811).

The third of the special promises complements the preceding two; it is intended for the dying and concerns the temporal aspect of dying, both when recited by the dying persons themselves, as well as when recited by others at the bedside of the dying. In revelation 66 the Lord Jesus says: "When hardened sinners recite this Chaplet, I will fill their soul with peace, and make happy the hour of their death" (Diary §1541). In the same revelation, Jesus directed a promise to all souls who will venerate The Divine Mercy: "They will experience no fear at the hour of death. My Mercy will shield them in this final struggle." In revelations concerning the Devotion "venerating The Divine Mercy" means "having trust in it." For this reason, if the Chaplet is to guarantee a peaceful and truly happy death, it is necessary to express internal trust in The Divine Mercy.

The fourth special promise widens the promise of this same grace of reciting the Chaplet at the bedside of the dying: "When this Chaplet is prayed at the bedside of the dying, I will place Myself between the Father and the soul of the dying person, not as a just judge but as a merciful Savior (Diary §1541).

The practical conclusion issuing from these great promises is self-evident: As long as the dying person has the ability to recite the Chaplet orally, let him do so. If he can no longer speak, let those keeping vigil at the bedside of the infirm person continue the prayer until the moment of death. Jesus himself directs the following appeal to priests: "Let priests present this Chaplet to sinners as a last resort" (Diary §687). We are all sinners as a result of the first fall. Therefore, let this Chaplet always be for us all, especially at the hour of death, a last resort.

THE HOUR OF DIVINE MERCY

Jesus himself referred to 3:00 in the afternoon, the hour of His death, as "the hour of great mercy toward the world." In revelation 59 He said: "At 3:00 o'clock implore My mercy especially for sinners; and, if only for a brief moment, steep yourself in My Passion, particular in My abandonment at the moment of agony. This is the hour of great mercy for the whole world. ...In this hour I will refuse nothing to the soul that makes a request of Me in virtue of My Passion" (Diary §1320).

Jesus put forth three conditions necessary for the prayers offered at the Hour of Divine Mercy to be heard. The prayer is to be directed to Jesus. It is to take place at 3:00 p.m., and it is to appeal to the value and merits of the Lord's Passion. To these, three other conditions should be added. From the very nature of every prayer, it follows that the object of the prayer must be in accordance with the will of God. The structure of the Devotion demands that the prayer be trustful, therefore steadfast, and in case of necessity, repeated time and again. As all forms of this Devotion, so also the Hour of Divine Mercy requires of its devotees the active practice of love of neighbor and works of mercy.

In the 68th revelation, Jesus instructed Sister Helen Faustina on how to celebrate the Hour of Divine Mercy (Diary 1572). All would do well to follow these instructions. Specifically, the Lord Jesus suggested that during this hour, Sister Helen Faustina beseech [Divine] Mercy for the entire world, especially for sinners. He encouraged her to meditate during this time on His Passion, particularly the aspect of His abandonment by all during His final agony. He attached the promise of understanding the meaning of His Passion to this meditation. He especially advised the Stations of the Cross. If time did not permit it, she should make a brief visit to the Sacred Heart of Jesus in the Most Blessed Sacrament. If this proved impossible, He requested that she immerse herself briefly in prayer.

PROPAGATION OF DEVOTION TO
THE DIVINE MERCY

Jesus considers the preaching of sermons about Divine Mercy to be on the same level with the propagation of devotion to the Divine Mercy by people who are not priests, in this respect: that He attaches identical promises to both. Revelations 19, 20, and 46 indicate as much: "Souls...who will glorify and proclaim My great Mercy to others will, at the hour of death, be dealt with according to My infinite Mercy," reads revelation 20 (Diary §379). Revelation 46 formulates His promise in this way: "Souls who propagate the honor of My Divine Mercy, I will protect throughout their entire lives as a loving mother does her infant and, at the hour of death, I will not be their Judge but a Merciful Savior" (Diary §1075).

Jesus, therefore, attached two promises to those who spread the veneration of The Divine Mercy: the first concerns one's entire life: it is Jesus' motherly care of the one who spreads this Devotion. The second concerns the hour of death: it is Jesus' assurance that in His attitude toward the dying His infinite Mercy will be manifested. Even though the formulation of both promises is not scientifically precise, nonetheless, it is strongly figurative and in general outlines shows that those who spread the veneration of The Divine Mercy can expect extraordinary Mercy at the hour of death.

Jesus attached particular pastoral efficacy to the sermons preached by priests about The Divine Mercy. In revelation 65, He told Helen Faustina: "Tell My priests that hardened sinners will crumble beneath their words when they speak of My unfathomable Mercy, of the compassion that I bear for them in My Heart" (Diary §1521). From these words it is evident that sermons will possess an extraordinary efficacy for the conversion of sinners precisely when their theme is the Mercy, Goodness and Compassion that Jesus has for sinners. Since a person's conversion to God is accomplished primarily in connection with the Sacrament of Penance, priests who have conversions at heart will actualize Jesus' urgent call by preaching about the Divine Mercy during retreats, spiritual exercises, and penitential services in preparation for sacramental confession. They will preach this Mercy well, however, if they themselves know it well; they will come to know it when they diligently meditate on the life, and particularly, the Passion of Jesus Christ.

Notes on the Translation of

Essential Features of the Devotion to The Divine Mercy

Robert Stackpole, S.T.D.

1. Emphases added. The Polish word here is "niewlasciwy" which literally means "improper." Given the pejorative connotations of this word in modern English, however, we have used the word "relative" instead, which is the traditional opposite of "proper" in Scholastic Theology, and which seems to preserve Fr. Rozycki's intended meaning. In Catholic theology, there are two basic types of honor: (1) "proper" which is given to a person, and (2) "relative" which is given to a thing associated with a person (e.g. to a picture of a loved one).

2. The Polish word here is "samoistna" which translates literally as "autonomous" religious worship. But such a phrase in English could easily cause confusion. An additional problem is that in the English-speaking world, "worship" has usually been considered appropriate only for God, whereas in Polish the same word "worship" can have several connotations, depending upon its context. Fr. Rozycki here divides "worship" into two types: "autonomous" religious worship directed to God alone, and acts of religious worship "directed to some created being." These two types correspond to two forms of "honor" discussed in traditional Scholastic Theology: (1) "latria" (English: worship or adoration) which is proper only to the uncreated God, and (2) "dulia" (English: veneration) which is proper to created excellence (man or angel). In order to avoid confusion for the reader we have used the word "supreme" or "supreme act" in place of "autonomous;" the student of Theology in the English speaking world might thereby more easily recognize that by "supreme" religious worship Fr. Rozycki means simply

"latria." Fr. Rozycki did not intend to create any novel theological jargon of his own in this essay, but merely tried to express in Polish these traditional Scholastic distinctions.

3. This traditional Polish title for God has no exact equivalent in English; closest to it might be the archaic English phrase "The Holy and Undivided Trinity."

4. Fr. Roczycki's reference here is incorrect. These words of Our Lord are found not in the initial revelation (Diary 47-48) but in one that occurred some time later (Diary §742).

5. This remains a controversial point, c.f. Diary §177 and §1486.

6. Fr. Rozycki's reference here is incorrect. The words actually are found in revelation no.58. See Fr. George W. Kosicki, C.S.B., Study Guide to the Diary of Blessed Faustina Kowalska (Stockbridge: Marian Helpers, 1996), 152.

7. The Polish literally has "novena." There may be an error in the original Polish publication, however, for "litany" seems clearly intended here, and the passage may refer to Diary entry §949.

8. On January 23rd, 1995, the Vatican Congregation for Divine Worship granted the bishops of Poland the right to celebrate the liturgical Feast of Divine Mercy on the Sunday after Easter, the very day Our Lord had requested for this celebration in his revelations to St. Faustina. At the canonization of St. Faustina on April 30, 2000, Pope John Paul II declared that from now on this Sunday will be known throughout the Church as "Divine Mercy Sunday."

9. The original Polish publication repeats the word for "redemption" here. Again, we suspect an error in the original, for "mercy" seems to be intended.

10. Several things should be noted about the Reverend Professor Rozycki's statement here:

— By "second Baptism" Prof. Rozycki does not mean a repetition of the sacrament, or some kind of additional baptism (as though an eighth sacrament), but a *renewal* of grace in the soul akin to that enjoyed as the result of the reception of the sacrament of Baptism. That this is Rev. Rozycki's meaning, is clear from the theological analysis of the contents of Sr. Faustina's spiritual *Diary* that he was requested to make, as a required step in canonization processes, to ascertain the integrity of the Catholic faith and Christian morals in the writings of a candidate for the honors of the altar.

— According to Jesus' promise, a person obtains the extraordinary grace of *the complete remission of sins and of the punishment due to them* by the worthy reception of Holy Communion on Mercy Sunday. It is *not* an *extra-sacramental* grace; it is intimately bound to the reception of the sacrament of the Body and Blood of Christ—the Eucharist. This is clearly implied in the professor's theological analysis mentioned above, as also in his text presented here, where the statement is made explicitly several times.

Thus, when Rev. Rozycki declares in this shorter treatise on the *Essential Features of the Devotion to The Divine Mercy*: "The exceptional grace of Divine Mercy Sunday is also greater than the graces of the other sacraments, with the exception of the Sacrament of Baptism," he does not mean to imply that the exceptional grace comes to us other than through the reception of Holy Communion on that day — rather, he is simply saying that ordinarily only the sacrament of Baptism effects in the soul the "complete forgiveness of sins and punishment." Reception of the Eucharist in the state of grace *ordinarily* remits only venial sin, while strengthening the soul against both venial and mortal sin (*Catechism*, 1394-1395). But on Mercy Sunday, according to Rev. Rozycki, based on Our Lord's words to St. Faustina, the reception of Holy Communion pours out upon a soul a complete renewal of baptismal grace.

Of course, this immediately raises the question of whether it is proper to the nature of the Eucharist to be the source of such an exceptional measure of grace. The answer is clear from the teachings of St. Thomas Aquinas and of the magisterium itself.

St. Thomas declares very clearly:

Moreover, not only are all the other sacraments ordered toward the Eucharist, but they produce their proper grace only in virtue of their relationship to the Eucharist. The Eucharist alone has of itself the power to confer grace, while the other sacraments confer grace only in virtue of the desire (votum) which their recipients have of receiving the Eucharist also.

St. Thomas elaborates further:

"This sacrament [of the Eucharist] has in itself the power to confer grace. No one has grace before receiving this sacrament except by a certain desire (*votum*) to receive it, the person's own desire in the case of an adult, or the Church's desire in the case of infants, as has been said above (*Summa*, III, q.73, art.3). Accordingly it is from the effectiveness of its power *that even from the mere desire to receive [this sacrament]* a person obtains grace whereby he is spiritually alive. Still it is true that when the sacrament itself is actually received, grace is increased and the spiritual life is perfected. ... It is by this sacrament, however, that grace is increased and the spiritual life is perfected, in order that man may be made perfect in himself through his being conjoined to God" (*Summa*, III, q. 79, art. I ad I. See also parallel passages).

This teaching is the foundation for the recommendation made by the Catechism of the Council of Trent to pastors of souls, when it obliges them to explain to the faithful what an abundance of riches is included in the mystery of the Eucharist (See: p.173, *Theological Dimension Of The Liturgy*, Cyprian

Vagaggini, O.S.B., The Liturgical Press, Collegeville, MN, 1976, from the 4th Italian Edition):

> This they will in some degree accomplish, if, having explained the efficacy and nature of all the sacraments, they compare the Eucharist to a fountain, the other sacraments to rivulets. For the Holy Eucharist is truly and necessarily to be called *the fountain of all graces*, containing as it does, after an admirable manner, the fountain itself of celestial gifts and graces, and the author of all the sacraments, Christ our Lord, from whom, as from its source, is derived whatever of goodness and perfection the other sacraments possess (Part 2, ch.4, n.47; in the translation by John A. McHugh and Charles J. Collan - *Catechism of the Council of Trent*, New York 1934, pp. 241-242).

The *Constitution on the Sacred Liturgy* of the Second Vatican Council re-echos this teaching: "Especially from the Eucharist, grace is poured forth upon us as from a fountain."

The centrality of the Eucharist as the fountain of all sacramental graces has also been clearly taught in the writings of great contemporary theologians. In *Theological Dimensions of the Liturgy,* for example, the great 20th century scholar Cyprian Vagaggini, OSB, argues persuasively that "the Eucharist, therefore [is the] sacrament and sacrifice, which realizes to the full the common notion and end of all the sacraments." He writes:

> All that has been said of the sacraments, that they are ordained to the Eucharistic sacrifice, can be said with even greater reason about all those rites in the liturgy which are of ecclesiastical institution: ceremonies, sacramentals, prayers, and especially the divine office. The basic reason is the same: we know that all these liturgical rites of ecclesiastical origin have no other aim than divine worship in Christ and the sanctification of man in Christ. Moreover, both of these categories exist only as participation in the sacrifice of Golgotha and as derivations from it, a sacrifice

which is continued sacramentally in the Mass. It is therefore only in the fact that they are dispositions, more or less immediate, to communion in the Eucharistic sacrifice, that all these rites have a significance.

Finally, we should bear in mind that theological analysis of Divine Mercy Sunday and of the extraordinary graces available on that day, has only just begun. In the future, no doubt, new perspectives will arise, both to extend the insights of Fr. Rozycki, and to supplement his work. For example, there is a theological tradition in the Church which states that a complete renewal of baptismal grace is available to the soul at *every sacramental confession*, if the soul comes to the Lord with perfect contrition, i.e., perfect love of God. St. Catherine of Siena, for example, writes in *The Dialogue* (no. 75) of how martyrdom, baptism by desire, and sacramental confession undertaken with a pure heart, all wash the soul as clean as baptism itself. Our Lord said to her:

> By shedding both blood and water I showed you the holy baptism of water that you receive through the power of my blood. But I was also showing you the baptism of blood, and this in two ways. The first touches those who are baptized in their own blood poured out for me. Though they could not have the other baptism, their own blood has power because of mine. Others are baptized in fire when they lovingly desire baptism but cannot have it. ...

> There is a second way the soul receives this baptism of blood, figuratively speaking. This my divine charity provided because I know how people sin because of their weakness. Not that weakness or anything else can force them to sin if they do not want to, but being weak they do fall into deadly sin and lose the grace they had drawn from the power of the blood in holy baptism. So my divine charity had to leave them an ongoing baptism of blood accessible by heartfelt contrition and a holy confession as

soon as they can confess to my ministers who hold the key to the blood. This blood the priest pours over the soul in absolution.

But if they cannot confess, heartfelt contrition is enough for the hand of my mercy to give them the fruit of this precious blood. ...

So you see, this baptism is ongoing, and the soul ought to be baptized in it right up to the end, in the way I have told you. In this baptism you experience that though my act of suffering on the cross was finite, the fruit of that suffering which you have received through me is infinite. This is because of the infinite divine nature joined with finite human nature [in Christ].

According to St. Catherine of Siena, therefore, the complete renewal of baptismal grace is available to the soul from the Mercy of God in a variety of ways, and a renewal of these graces should be a constant feature of the life of the soul journeying toward perfection.

If this be so, then what is so "extraordinary" about the grace of baptismal renewal offered to souls on Divine Mercy Sunday? Is not such an extraordinary grace always available to us?

First, let us examine the nature of the extraordinary grace itself.

One can, theoretically, receive the complete remission of sins and punishment any time from the sacrament of Confession followed by Holy Communion, all undertaken with the perfect love of God. *But how many of the faithful ordinarily receive these sacraments with such a pure disposition?* Usually, the intentions of the penitent-communicant are more mixed, including fear of God as well as love, and, to some extent, with continuing attachment to their sins. As a result, while their sins are forgiven, there remains the temporal punishment due to sin (see

Catechism 1472-1473). Of course, this temporal punishment can be completely taken away through a plenary indulgence, granted by the Church, through the devout performance of certain designated good works (such as the recitation of prayers, giving of alms, visiting a shrine, etc.) — but, again, if these works are not undertaken with pure love of God, then the indulgence is only partial, not plenary. The *complete* remission of sins *and* punishment, *ex opere operato*, is *ordinarily* only available to the soul at baptism. What Jesus Christ has promised to the world, through St. Faustina, is that this complete renewal of this same baptismal grace — the complete remission of *sins* and punishment — is also available to the faithful through the reception in a state of grace of Holy Communion on Divine Mercy Sunday.

In other words, one could argue that what makes Mercy Sunday so extraordinary is not just the *eminence* of the graces offered, but also, uniquely, the *lesser requirement* for receiving them: the reception of Holy Communion by a heart filled only with trust in Divine Mercy. This "trust," it might be said, is not yet an act of perfect love of God, not yet perfect contrition. For trust in God involves merely a cleaving to God because of His promised benefits. As such, it is, merely, a precondition for the formation, by divine grace, of perfect love in the soul: the pure, selfless love of God for His own sake. Trust is the opening of the soul by faith, hope, humility, and repentance, to receive all the most eminent graces — and especially the gift of perfect charity — from the Heart of the Savior. Fr. Rozycki describes trust in this way:

> This same attitude of life is described by St. Paul and by the whole of Christian theology as hope, the divine virtue of hope which springs from a living faith in the infinity of God's love and goodness towards us. It is indissolubly tied to humility, that is the sincere and deep conviction that all good within us and which we do is the work and gift of God; that we possess nothing except that which we have

from God. This trust-hope constitutes the opening of a soul's receiving Divine grace, and the requesting of it is an attitude of continuous and most effective prayer.

Truly, this very disposition — trust, and nothing more — is what the Lord asks us to bring to Divine Mercy Sunday, in order to receive the whole ocean of His mercy (Diary entries 1520, and 1578):

I have opened My Heart as a living fountain of mercy. Let all souls draw life from it. Let them approach this sea of mercy with great trust. ... The more a soul trusts, the more it will receive.

Still, one might well ask: why are the "floodgates" of Divine Mercy said to be fully open, on this basis, only on one particular Feast Day, rather than at every Holy Communion?

This objection seems much like the objection of some of the radical Protestant reformers of the 16th and 17th centuries to the claim that Holy Communion imparts special graces to souls, in a unique and more intimate manner than is normally available to souls from the practice of communal prayer. Why do we limit God's Mercy in this way? The answer is that we do not intend to limit God's Mercy — He is always free to pour out His Mercy in any way, at any time — but we do intend to believe His promises. From Holy Scripture we know that the Father promised that a unique and intimate communion with His Son can be obtained through the Holy Eucharist, and from Christ's prophetic revelations to St. Faustina, we know that He has promised an exceptional abundance of graces — a complete renewal of Baptism — to those who receive Holy Communion in the state of grace, with great trust in His Mercy, on Divine Mercy Sunday. This is not because Christ is "stingy," or withholds such a plenary grace at other times, but because His own divine way is to bestow His graces in a manner and time which best enables us to receive them. For example, to creatures made up of soul and body, He willed to impart spiritual graces in a bodily manner: through consecrated, transubstantiated bread and wine. The manner of the gift was thereby suited to the nature and needs of its intended recipients. Similarly, to souls struggling to accept the Love of Christ, and to love Him in return (that is, to all of us) our Lord promised that the most extraordinary graces of His Mercy could be obtained merely through reception of Holy Communion, with trust in The Divine Mercy, at the very time — indeed on the very day — in the liturgical cycle best suited to maximize and predispose souls to trust in Him: the culmination and summary of the celebration of the Paschal Mystery, the very Octave Day of Easter.

III.
The Road to Canonization

by Rev. Seraphim Michalenko, MIC, STL, SEOL

with Mary Ann McSweeny

Introduction

Helen Kowalska (1905-1938), a simple, God-centered woman with little education and from a poor Polish family, is now known throughout the world as St. Faustina, the Apostle of Divine Mercy. Once again God works through a little person to make known the Good News of His unconditional love for all of humanity. Once again Jesus searches out one of the least of our brothers and sisters to spread the message of God's boundless mercy for each and every member of our human family.

We are all beloved children of God, called to serve our Lord with the gifts and talents we have been given, and according to the circumstances of our lives. We are all called to holiness, and St. Faustina is one of our great models for how to respond to that call with all our hearts, all our souls, all our minds, and all our strength. As the special messenger reminding us of Jesus' mercy, St. Faustina touches our hearts with a gentle firmness that helps us to transform our ordinary lives into extraordinary lives of love and mercy in service to God and each other.

Through the example of her life, St. Faustina teaches us to place total reliance on God and to surrender all that we are and do to His loving guidance and mercy. She teaches us how to be in God's presence with all the innocence and faith of a tiny child. She teaches us to be in a partnership of love with God as we move through our lives on the road to holiness.

The Merciful Way

Jesus is the way to everlasting life with God, yet the road to holiness can be as individual as we are. St. Faustina has placed clear markers for us to follow on the merciful way to God's kingdom. Her example teaches us the merciful way to oneness with God. Her mission as the Apostle of Divine Mercy assures us that the merciful way is accessible to all of God's children.

Mercy is the fruit of God's unconditional, overflowing, unending love for us. When we choose to walk with St. Faustina on the merciful way, we surrender the burdens we carry to our Lord and open our lives and our hearts to receive God's compassion, forgiveness, and loving kindness.

Jesus experienced every kind of hardship in His life: He was a refugee; He lived in a country ruled by oppressive leaders; He was rejected by His own people; He was betrayed; He was beaten; He was condemned as a common criminal; He was abandoned by His closest friends; He was a victim of the death penalty. Jesus knows the hardships that we face as frail human persons. He knows that we experience pain, depression, addictions, loneliness, prejudice, grief, illness, and death. He wants to share even our misery with us. That is the merciful way that St. Faustina shows us.

The merciful way was St. Faustina's road to holiness; it can be ours, too. When we are willing to ask for and receive Jesus' mercy, He is free to work in our lives to heal us and make us whole and holy. When we experience the Lord's mercy, our lives are transformed. We are empowered to act mercifully to others: to feed the hungry, clothe the naked, visit the sick and imprisoned, speak out against injustice, and to spread the good news of Divine Mercy by our own life witness.

The road to holiness is a pilgrimage for everyone. The wonder of St. Faustina is that in following the merciful way, she so completely gave herself to Jesus that He could work marvels through her, and continues to answer the petitions she places before Him. The merciful way became St. Faustina's road to canonization.

The Three Steps of Mercy

Creation

The Triune God is a unified community of love that is, always was, and always will be. Creation is the fruit of that love, the merciful response of God to the cry of Nothingness: "Let us be!" God answered by creating the universe and all that it contains, with the human person as the pinnacle of all of God's creation. Creation, then, is the first step of mercy.

God works in partnership with us to create new human life. Throughout the history of salvation, God has responded with mercy to those who have not been able to conceive children. For example, Sarah and Elizabeth, two devout women of our faith tradition, were barren. They turned the energy of their grief into constant prayer, and God's merciful response was to bless Sarah with her son, Isaac, and Elizabeth with her son, John. In addition, God chose these dearly wanted children to play important roles in the history of salvation.

In a similar scenario, for the first ten years of their marriage, Stanislaus and Marianna Kowalski, Helen's parents, knew the grief of not being able to conceive a child. From the time of their marriage, they prayed unceasingly to be blessed with children. Madame Babel, Marianna's mother, joined in their prayer, offering up this intention at the Holy Sacrifice of Mass as well. She encouraged her daughter to trust in God's mercy and assured her that she would have children.

In fact, Marianna ended up giving birth to ten children! Josephine, the eldest, was born after an extremely prolonged and difficult labor. Genevieve, their second daughter, was born about two years later after another complicated childbirth. Marianna was very nervous during the third pregnancy, but little Helen was born without any problems, and the births of the seven children who followed Helen were also remarkably trouble-free, although two daughters died in infancy. In later years, Marianna said that little Helen's birth "sanctified my womb."

Called into being by the merciful response of a loving God to the fervent and wholehearted prayers of her parents and grandmother, Helen's creation was the beginning of the road to canonization for St. Faustina. And as her life went on — and after she died — it became more and more clear that this young woman had been blessed with particular gifts to use to remind the world of God's love and mercy for us all.

Redemption

Because humanity broke the relationship with God that was begun when we were created in God's own image and likeness, the need for redemption — or mercy — became imperative. God's mercy reaches out to us to restore that broken relationship, that separation caused by our own arrogance, pride, selfishness, and greed. God redeems us to heal and make whole that which God created in the first place.

Jesus died once for all. Redemption is ours. Yet in our individual lives we continue to sin. We continue to break that relationship of love entrusted to us — entrusted to human persons, God's highest form of creation. Therefore, there is a daily need to examine our consciences, to make amends to those we have hurt, to forgive those who hurt us, and to surrender our lives to God's loving care. This is the work of a lifetime, and only when we work in partnership with God is redemption, the second step of mercy, possible.

The milieu into which Helen Kowalska was born seems to have helped her to enjoy an extraordinarily unbroken relationship with God. Some two years before she was born, two boys of her parish claimed to have seen the face of Jesus, His head crowned with thorns, in the Eucharist during the 40 Hours Devotion. People from all around came to see this miraculous sight, and the crowds were so great and excited to be there that they actually did physical damage to the buildings. However, when the bishop's delegation made an examination of the situation and the evidence, they concluded that it was only the shadows from the candles that created the illusion of Jesus' face in the Eucharist. Despite this official ruling, people still came to the parish church in the hopes of seeing a vision of Jesus.

Helen was born into this village where there was ongoing excitement about Jesus' presence in the Blessed Sacrament. She undoubtedly felt that fervor and it likely shaped her own deep connection and devotion to the Eucharist.

Helen was also born into a family where God was central. As he did early morning chores, her father sang "Godzinki," the traditional Little Hours of the Immaculate Conception. During Lent he substituted "Gorzkie Zale," the Lamentations of the Lord's Passion. He also liked to sing a hymn of praise, the "Kiedy Ranne."

Stanislaus read his children stories of the desert fathers, fascinating Helen who recounted these same stories to the children of the village. Helen wanted very much to model her life on the lives of these holy people. In later years, she learned that there were religious orders where everyday life was centered around God, and she aspired to join such an order.

From the time little Helen was three or four, she told her parents and older sisters that the Blessed Virgin Mary appeared to her in dreams, taking her into a beautiful garden. Her family did not quite believe her, yet they knew her to be a very truthful girl. It seems one more indication that Helen's relationship with God and the saints was very special. It seems a strong indication, too, that God's mercy was constantly at work in Helen's life, calling her to be restored to oneness with God.

The road to holiness, however, is not always straight, but often spirals. Although Helen felt the call to holiness and had a special relationship with Mary, still there were obstacles to her maturing desire to devote her life to God as a religious sister. The most serious obstacle was her family; they were opposed to her leaving them for the religious life. They cited their poverty and inability to provide a dowry as their principle reason. A dowry was intended to help support the religious community, or to provide financial assistance to a young woman who was not able to take final vows and had to return to the secular world. Helen said to them, "But He promised me that He would take care of all my needs." It seems clear that she meant Jesus.

Helen's family held firm to their conviction that unless they provided a dowry for her, Helen could not become a religious sister. Helen, in obedience to them, went along with their decision for quite some time. In fact, she determined to devote herself to the pleasures of the secular life.

With this attitude, Helen attended a dance in 1924. Suddenly as she was dancing, she saw Jesus, stripped and covered with wounds. He said to her, "How long must I wait for you?" She walked off the dance floor and sat down in a daze, telling her sister Josephine that she had a headache. Then she made her way to the cathedral where she fell prostrate in the form of a cross in front of the tabernacle, saying to the Lord, "What will you have me do?" The Lord answered that she must go to Warsaw where she would enter a convent.

At the end of her prayer, Helen bought a couple of cookies and a little bottle of whisky for her uncle. She went to his house and gave them to him, asking that he take her to the train station so she could go to Warsaw to find the religious order Jesus wanted her to join. Years later a religious sister who knew her at the time of the dance said, "Is that what happened to her?" She had seen Helen acting as if she were stunned at the dance and then Helen disappeared without a trace from the local scene.

Helen answered the enormous grace of hearing Jesus call to her with immediate action, an unconditional *yes*. God shows no partiality; we are each called to be one with God. Yet none of us responds in exactly the same way. Helen's wholehearted response to Jesus was indicative of her great spiritual gifts, her deep desire to be with God, and her gratitude for God's mercy and for the gift of redemption.

Helen's uncle observed her crying on the train as she left her family to do what Jesus asked of her. He interpreted her grief as sadness at leaving her family behind, without saying goodbye to her parents whom she loved dearly. Perhaps, too, Helen was feeling grief at her human frailty and weakness in light of the perfect love and patience of Divine Mercy being shown to her.

The Image of The Divine Mercy that St. Faustina caused to be painted has rays of two colors — for blood and for water. Because Jesus shed His blood for our redemption, it makes sense to explore the chemistry of blood to understand the idea of redemption. Blood cleanses, taking out the toxins that get into our bodies, the things that make us ill or keep us out of balance. And blood also gives us life, bringing oxygen and nutrients to all the parts of our body so that we may be healthy. Mercy — redemption — is therefore a part of a purification process that enables us to understand the attitudes and behaviors that throw us out of balance spiritually or prevent us from being with God. Once we are aware of these attitudes and behaviors, we begin to work with God to be transformed and have new life with and in God. For St. Faustina, a key cleansing aspect of her personal redemption was in letting go of the obstacle that her family represented. The new, healthy life was turning her will and her whole life over to the care of Jesus. Her complete acceptance of Jesus' mercy allowed her to move further along the road to canonization.

Sanctification

Sanctification, or deification, is the third step of mercy. This is the merciful gesture of God that allows us to be holy as God is holy, and only as God is holy. Deification is our participation in God by God's permission.

The canonization of St. Faustina seems to make her deification obvious, yet it was the road she traveled during her lifetime that helped to form her in holiness for participation in God. God gives us free will so that we might deliberately choose to do His will during our lifetime. God's will as expressed in the Gospel is to love God with all our heart, soul, mind, and strength; to love our neighbor as ourselves; to forgive and be reconciled with one another; to respond to violence with peace; and to confront the darkness of evil with the light of love.

A part of the message that St. Faustina shares with us is that Jesus wants us to show mercy to each other through deeds of mercy that come from hearts filled with the love of God. In our faith tradition we have what are called Works of Mercy, which carry out the will of God in various ways. The Spiritual Works of Mercy are admonishing sinners, instructing the uninformed, counseling the doubtful, comforting the sorrowful, bearing wrongs patiently, forgiving offenses, and praying for the living and the dead. The Corporal Works of Mercy are feeding the hungry and giving drink to the thirsty, clothing the naked, sheltering the homeless, comforting the imprisoned, visiting the sick, and burying the dead.

Unless our deeds of mercy are the fruit of our love for one another, they are merely a kind of detached social service. Followers of Christ act mercifully when we understand the great gift of God's mercy in our own lives and wish to share that mercy with others. If her deeds of mercy are any indication, St. Faustina showed a profound understanding of God's dynamic presence in her life even as a girl. For example, she would get up several times during the night to pray. Her mother remonstrated with her, saying, "Go back to sleep or you'll lose your mind." But Helen answered, "I think it's my angel calling me to pray." Helen seemed to understand the deep need for constant prayer in what is still a troubled world.

Stanislaus Kowalski dealt severely towards his children in terms of punishment, even for minor transgressions. Helen, because of her mild nature and easy obedience to her parents, was almost never the object of this kind of punishment. However, she would often step between her father and whichever sister or brother was about to be whipped. She seemed to know that the answer to violence was peace, and she seemed to have an instinct to protect the weak. She would also gently admonish her sisters and brothers to practice obedience so as not to provoke their father.

Although Helen's family was very poor, still people would come to their door begging for food. Helen would intercede on their behalf with her mother so that they would not go away empty-handed. On some occasions, elderly women would come to the door begging for alms for the poor in exchange for which they promised to pray for the family. Again Helen would intercede for them, and one time, when she was about twelve years old, she dressed up like these women and went door-to-door begging for alms for the poor, promising prayers in return. Her own sister said that Helen was so convincing that she did not even recognize her! Helen turned the alms she had begged over to the parish priest to distribute to the poor.

Helen thought of other creative ways to help the poor and needy. One time she devised a kind of lottery — people in the neighborhood donated simple trinkets and she sold tickets to be drawn to win the donated goods. Again she gave the parish priest the few pennies she earned from the lottery to help those in need.

Generous, innovative, compassionate toward the poor and weak, constantly at prayer: Helen's girlhood was the beginning of the road to sanctification. She seemed to relish finding a variety of ways to help others. She seemed to keep her eyes open to find new and different ways to act on the behalf of the poor. She seemed spontaneously to act mercifully, reaching out in understanding and compassion to those in need.

Given our human frailty and weakness, we only hope to emulate God's holiness in this life. The more we practice simple, heartfelt deeds of mercy, however, the more we are comfortable with sharing God's gifts of love and mercy with those around us. God's grace calls us to participate in His mission of mercy. When we are given the grace to respond, as St. Faustina did, we grow in holiness and hope to enjoy — as St. Faustina enjoys — glorification… sanctification… the holiness of God with God and in God.

The Three Qualities to Practice

Humility

When Helen went to Warsaw at Jesus' direction, she prayed to Mary, Jesus' mother for protection and guidance. Of all the guidance Mary gave Helen, perhaps the most important was the list of qualities Helen needed to practice in order to deepen her spiritual life and to grow in holiness. "I desire, my dearly beloved daughter, that you practice the three virtues that are dearest to me — and most pleasing to God. The first is humility, humility, and once again humility; the second virtue, purity; the third virtue, love of God" (*Diary of St. Maria Faustina Kowalska*, #1415).

Humility… humility… humility: obviously a special virtue to practice! Yet so many people mistakenly associate humility with humiliation. Humiliation is an unhealthy, shame-based reaction to being the object of someone's anger, fear, indifference, or desire to control. Humility, on the other hand, is a state of being that is honest, self-accepting, and receptive to God's healing and grace.

True humility is being able to look at ourselves honestly and see ourselves as we really are: our faults, our goodness, our weaknesses, our strengths, our defects, our talents, our short-comings, our gifts. True humility seeks to know who we are in the context of love and mercy. True humility sees who we are in all of our human frailty in the light of God's infinite perfection — and allows us to accept ourselves, just as we are, as beloved children of God.

True humility does not judge or condemn. True humility is not indifferent or prejudiced towards others. True humility sees that we are all equally precious in the eyes of God, and that each of us is blessed with particular gifts to accomplish what God needs us to accomplish during our lifetime.

True humility lets us follow the path that God has chosen for us without fear of what others may think of us. True humility allows us to trust God, even when God's way for us seems risky or lonely or puzzling.

Helen's great desire was to join a religious order in order to grow in perfection. However, her family's objections distracted her from that path until Jesus asked why she was keeping Him waiting. This was a great lesson in humility for Helen. She saw herself in the light of Jesus' perfection and knew that she, in her humanity, had let Him down.

From that point forward, Helen became totally receptive and available to God, moving around any obstacle that might prevent her from continuing on the road to holiness. For example, when she interviewed with Mother Michael Moraczewska, the Mother Superior of the Sisters of Our Lady of Mercy in Warsaw, Helen had no money to pay for the clothing she would need in the religious life. Helen moved around this obstacle by following Mother Michael's sugges-tion to work and save a few hundred *zlotys*. She saved the money within a year, much to Mother Michael's surprise, and was admitted to the novitiate on August 1, 1925.

In the convent of the Sisters of Our Lady of Mercy, Sister Faustina (as Helen was called from the time she received the habit and veil) was given the most lowly of tasks: working in the kitchen or the vegetable garden, acting as porter. She was not well educated, having had only a couple of years of formal schooling. The notebooks of her diary are full of misspellings and errors in punctuation. Yet what shines out is her willingness to love and serve the Lord as she was gifted and as she was called. This is a sign of the humility she practiced.

Even in the simple positions she held in the convent, sometimes Sister Faustina was asked to do things that were beyond her capabilities and knowledge. Humility allowed her to accept her limitations, and she knew to turn to Jesus for help in accomplishing what needed to be done. Once, fairly early on in her life in the convent, Sister Faustina was left in charge of the kitchen while the sisters who normally ran the kitchen were off the premises with other duties. On that hot August day, at a time in history when refrigeration was unavailable, someone donated a whole cow, ready to be butchered, to the convent. Sister Faustina had no butchering skills and did not know much about preserving meat. The other kitchen helpers knew even less than she.

Instead of panicking, Sister Faustina instructed the other sisters to help her finish the chores that they did know how to do. Then, because she knew her limitations, she had them all go into the convent chapel where they prayed in front of the Blessed Sacrament for guidance with dealing with the cow.

God is so good and merciful! Even in a matter as seemingly trivial as this, God immediately answered Faustina's plea for help. Upon returning to the kitchen, she directed the butchering and preserving of the meat according to God's guidance. When the sister who usually was in charge of the kitchen and food preparation examined the work, she said that Faustina had done exactly what she herself would have done. In fact, the meat was so well preserved that none of it went bad, and the sisters were able to make good use of it all.

St. Faustina shows us that we work in partnership with God on the road to holiness. When we acknowledge our limitations, we admit our need for God. Humility teaches us that we can do nothing apart from God. Yet we cannot just expect God to take care of our problems; we must also be willing to do our part by discerning God's will for us and following it to the best of our ability.

The words that Jesus instructed Faustina to have placed on the Image of The Divine Mercy are "Jesus, I trust in you!" Perhaps the most important part of practicing humility is learning to trust that God is always present to us, always there to listen to us, and always ready to help us. We are fragile human persons who make mistakes and do mean-spirited things — and yet Jesus is always there for us, waiting to forgive us, waiting to heal us, waiting to welcome us home. Jesus is there ready to ease our burdens of pain, grief, anxiety, fear, illness, loneliness, and abandonment. Jesus is there reaching out to us in mercy from a heart burning with love for each and every one of us. To act upon this understanding is to practice humility.

Knowing that we, in light of God's perfection, are so imperfect, and believing that God loves us nonetheless — this is the height of humility. St. Faustina, on the road to canonization, leads us to this height with her own example of going to Jesus in times of need, however mundane or trivial those needs may have seemed, trusting that He is reaching out in mercy to heal and to help.

Purity

The second quality that our Blessed Mother encouraged St. Faustina to cultivate was purity, further explained by our Lord as purity of intention. Although the process of purification is linked to God's grace and our response to God's grace, still there are endless opportunities for us to make the choice to practice purity and purity of intention on the road to holiness.

Once again, St. Faustina provides us with a living model.

Although it is tempting to limit purity's scope to the physical, in fact, purity goes far beyond this. It is extremely important to note, however, that St. Faustina's vocation was as a virgin, a woman religious dedicated body, soul, and heart to our Lord. She delighted in her vocation and was convinced that God holds a special place for those whose gifts include voluntary celibacy in service to the Lord. Her complete contentment and joy with her vocation and gifts makes St. Faustina an inspiring example for us as we struggle to discern our own vocations and gifts.

St. Faustina was decidedly not a one-dimensional person, however, and she brought the quality of purity to the whole of her life from the time of her childhood. Until World War I, the section of Poland where Helen lived was under the oppressive rule of the Russians. An indication of the gravity of the oppression was that the Russians prohibited the Polish people from conducting schools in their own language, and so for most Poles in that sector of the country there was no formal education. Once the war was under way, however, Russian rule was dismantled, and the people started to school their children in Polish. Starting in 1917 Helen went to school for three terms, beginning in the second grade since she had learned to read at home. However, in order to make room for younger children, she and other older children had to leave school in 1919.

During this brief period of formal education, Helen demonstrated the purity of deed and intention that marked her life in general. She took positive advantage of the educational opportunities being offered to her, and devoted herself to her studies with zest and dedication. She even won a school prize by doing a fine recitation of Adam Mickiewicz's poem "Powrot Taty" ("Daddy's Return Home"). Her teacher was very sorry that Helen had to leave school, feeling that she showed great promise.

Although her time in school was limited, Helen made good use of it. She showed gratitude for the chance to better herself, and made intelligent use of the time she had to learn as much as possible. At the time, Helen had no idea that the diaries she would write would have such an effect on the entire world. The way she applied herself to her studies was simply the sign of a pure intention to grow in wisdom, understanding, and learning.

In light of St. Faustina's example, it makes sense for us to examine our own attitudes towards education, and how we make use of the educational opportunities offered to us. As we follow St. Faustina's path on the road to canonization, we realize more fully that her pilgrimage was not for her benefit alone. She teaches us so much with her own choices and continual gratitude for the opportunities that God sent her way. She offers us a unique education in purity and holiness.

Work is another area where St. Faustina consciously integrated the practice of purity. After she had to leave school to make way for younger children, Helen worked at home for a time, then asked her parents to let her go out to work as a servant as her older sisters had done. She was not quite 15 years old, but they agreed, finding her a situation with a neighbor's sister near Lodz. She stayed there for about a year, working as a housemaid and taking care of the young son of the family – who, as a man in his nineties, reminisced sitting on her lap and having her tell him stories.

Helen's employers had a bakery. On one occasion, while she was in the courtyard of the bakery, she had another vision of "lights," as she called them. This time they must have been intense because she screamed, "Fire!" Although a doctor was called and gave her medications for this so-called hallucination, Helen indicated to her sister, who was sent to see her, that she was not losing her mind, but that she would not remain there for long; she had to enter a convent.

Her parents would not hear of her desire to pursue a religious vocation, and so Helen moved to Lodz where she lived for a time with her uncle's family and continued to work as before.

She held several positions as a servant and seemed to give satisfaction wherever she worked. She refused her services, however, to any family that she felt did not live a Christian life. Helen even set the terms of employment in one position with three women who belonged to the Third Order of St. Francis: she would accept a modest salary, but insisted that she be allowed to attend daily Mass, have free time to visit the sick and pray for the dying, and that the women's chaplain become her confessor. With her attention to details about her work situations, Helen again showed that the practice of purity was integral to her everyday life.

Sometimes work engrosses all of our life and we become workaholics, neglecting our families, our health, and our God. St. Faustina teaches us that our work must be an opportunity for us to practice purity of intention and holiness as we seek to uphold the Gospel imperatives – love of God, neighbor, and self; taking care of the poor and needy; choosing peace over violence; serving all with whom we come in contact with kindness.

Always, no matter what job she held, Helen's desire was to enter a convent. While she was working for the three women, she was under the care of a priest who told her that she needed to be confirmed if she wanted to enter the religious life, and so she made the necessary preparation and received the sacrament.

Purity of thought, purity of attitude, purity of behavior, purity of intention: St. Faustina's example helps us to transform our negative patterns of living. She teaches us to center our thoughts on God's command to love one another, helping us to see everyone we meet as a living icon of God, as a precious and beloved child of God. She helps us to change our attitudes, showing us how to eliminate indifference and lack of trust from our interactions with God and others. She leads us to choose actions that are based in loving kindness, compassion, and mercy. She shows us how to act from motives that are untainted with selfishness or greed, so that we intend always to do God's will to the best of our ability.

Purity is a quality that renews our innocence. St. Faustina put her entire life into God's loving hands with a child-like faith and trust. Without cultivating purity, the innocence of wonder, of delight in God's creation, of joy in God's mercy is not possible. St. Faustina opened her heart in pure innocence to allow Jesus to use her as an instrument to remind the world of Divine Mercy.

Love of God

The third quality that Mary asked Helen to practice was love of God. Jesus tells us that the first and greatest commandment is to love God with all our hearts, all our souls, all our minds, and all our strength. Since God *is* love, any time we love — ourselves, others, or any of God's creatures or creations — we are practicing love of God. Most of us are asked to love in little ways, to bring an attitude of love to the events and people that make up our lives. Again St. Faustina's life inspires us to find small ways to practice enormous love for God.

As with most practices, seeing loving kindness modeled at home helps us to act in a similar way. Helen's mother set a good example of love for her children. For instance, every day Marianna brought a hot lunch to Stanislaus wherever he happened to be working as a carpenter. She made good use of the walk home to gather wood for the family fire. As a general rule, when it was a question of discipline, her sons remembered that she tempered the father's severity with understanding compassion. Yet Stanislaus, too, modeled love for God for his family by his hard work on their behalf, his heartfelt ritual of daily prayer, and his cherished practice of reading stories of monks and hermits to the children. Helen seems to have cultivated a similar disposition of ready willingness to help others and show loving kindness towards her family and other people — as well as the animals that came under her care.

From earliest childhood Helen seemed to have a sense that unless God was at the center of her life, life was meaningless.

She seemed to deliberately seek opportunities to improve her conscious contact with God in order to discern God's will for her, to give thanks for all that God did for her, and to open her heart to be an instrument of God's love and mercy in the world.

The family was so poor that Josephine, Genevieve, and Helen shared one good dress among them, and had to take turns attending Sunday Mass. On the Sundays when she had to stay at home, Helen would go into the garden and read from a prayerbook while Mass was going on. Even when her mother called to her to come help, Helen would not respond. When she knew that the celebration of the Eucharist had finished, Helen would go to her mother and ask for forgiveness. "I have to do my duty to God first," she would explain.

During the preparation for making her First Communion, she became aware that attending Mass was essential to her spiritual life. Somehow three dresses were found so that all of the older girls could attend Sunday Mass. She had a great devotion to the Blessed Sacrament, and during her night prayers would face in the direction of a church where the Blessed Sacrament was reserved.

St. Faustina's life teaches us that to answer God's call to holiness, we must make God our priority and balance our inner prayer life with deeds of mercy. When she was about seven she attended a Vespers service where, before the Blessed Sacrament, she promised her life to Jesus and created a special "cell" inside her heart where she could go to be with Jesus in quiet. The strength she drew from this contemplative prayer life enabled her to serve God actively, working cheerfully, speaking kindly to others, responding with compassion to those in need, and seeking the face of Jesus in everyone she met.

Love of God is also love of truth. In many ways we dodge the truth about ourselves, refusing to shine the light of honesty on our lives, preferring to remain in denial about those moral shortcomings that keep us apart from God. Helen had a deep love for the truth, seeking to know herself better in relationship to God. Her acts of obedience to her parents, her willingness to ask for forgiveness, her attention to education and work, her love of children and the fun she had with them: all of these are signs of a person at home with herself, a person who is not afraid to be fully alive and human, a person who knows the ultimate truth: that she is a beloved child of God.

Sometimes Helen's gift for the truth made her interpret even jokes literally. Once when she was little, her father teasingly told her that she was really the daughter of a neighbor. She packed her few belongings and started to walk down the road to the home where she thought she truly belonged. Her mother explained to her that her father spoke in jest and brought her back. Her family interpreted Helen's leaving home to her being unable to believe her father would not speak the truth.

When she was a postulant with the Sisters of Our Lady of Mercy, one of her former employers was asked to come to Warsaw to give a reference for her. By mistake her employer went to the wrong convent, and explained that she was there to give a testimonial for Helen, a former housemaid. The portress said that they did not take housemaids as postulants (house-maids had a reputation for being careless and untrustworthy) and that Helen must have lied to enter the convent. Her employer flew to her defense, saying, "Helen would never lie to me, if I could not believe her, I would never believe any-one else!" She was totally convinced of Helen's goodness and adherence to the truth.

When she finally found the convent of the Sisters of Our Lady of Mercy, Helen's employer told them of Helen's love for the truth and how she would never expect Helen not to tell the truth. She also told of the way Helen would sing about the Blessed Sacrament as she worked, showing that her mind was on Jesus, and that her work was being offered up for God's glory.

In such simple ways, St. Faustina reminds us that love of God is a daily willingness to surrender to God's perfect will, letting go of our own need to be in control; a daily willingness to spend time in prayer with God, seeking out moments of solitude to keep God at the center of our lives and to keep us grounded in God's gentle strength and enduring wisdom; a daily willingness to shine the light of truth on our personal shortcomings, trusting that God will help us to transform our lives; a daily willingness to reach out to our neighbors in compassion and respect, helping those in need, especially the poor.

As we practice love of God in our daily lives, we follow St. Faustina more surely on the merciful way.

The Road to Canonization

The road to canonization for St. Faustina was the process of being created, redeemed, and brought by God to the heights of sanctity. She was created in mercy by God, the fruit of God's love in response to her parents' earnest prayer; a beloved daughter born to parents who longed for children; a precious child of God destined to walk the merciful way back home to God, leading scores of other pilgrims by the example of her life.

Jesus, The Divine Mercy, our Redeemer and Brother, called constantly to Faustina, asking her to completely surrender her life and will to God. She was given the grace to hear His call, and the grace to respond with passion and dedication. She centered her life in God, searching out anything that might block an intimate relationship with our Lord. With patience and great trust, she opened her heart to let God's healing touch transform any attitude, thought, or behavior that might keep her from unity with Him

Through her willing and constant practice of humility, purity, and love of God, St. Faustina grew in holiness, ever hopeful that God's mercy would further perfect her in holiness as God is holy.

St. Faustina's life here among us was her road to canonization, and by her own example, she teaches us the deep faith of knowing not that Jesus *can* hear us, but that Jesus *does* hear us, however trivial our needs may seem. She teaches us to hand the burdens of our problems and misery over to Jesus who, in love and mercy, waits to receive them. She teaches us how to put our lives into God's loving hands with the simple confidence of a child who knows it is dearly loved. She teaches us that we are partners in love and mercy with God as we make our way home to God. She teaches us that the road to canonization starts here, now.